HEIRS *of the* KING

Other Discovery House Titles by Warren W. Wiersbe

Bless You: Receiving and Sharing the Blessings of the Lord
The Lost Shepherd: Finding and Keeping the Right Pastor
The New Pilgrim's Progress with notes by Warren W. Wiersbe
Who Am I?: New Testament Pictures of the Christian Life

HEIRS
of the

KING

LIVING *the* BEATITUDES

WARREN W. WIERSBE

DISCOVERY HOUSE
PUBLISHERS®

Previously published as *Live Like a King*.

Discovery House Publishers is affiliated with RBC Ministries,
Grand Rapids, Michigan.

Discovery House books are distributed to the trade exclusively by
Barbour Publishing, Inc., Uhrichsville, Ohio.

Requests for permission to quote from this book should be directed to:
Permissions Department, Discovery House Publishers, P.O. Box 3566,
Grand Rapids, MI 49501.

Library of Congress Cataloging-in-Publication Data

Wiersbe, Warren W.
[Live like a king]
Heirs of the king : living the Beatitudes / Warren W. Wiersbe.
p. cm.
Originally published: Chicago : Moody Press, c1976.
ISBN: 1-57293-215-5
1. Beatitudes. I. Title.

BT382.W53 2007
241.5'3—dc22   2007004585

Interior design by Sherri L. Hoffman

Printed in the United States of America

10 11 12/ VP /7 6 5 4 3

Dedicated to
DON AND KATHY BOWMAN

whose friendship, expertise and
prayers have encouraged us greatly,
and we thank you.

Warren and Betty Wiersbe

CONTENTS

PREFACE

These chapters are based on a series of messages I delivered at Moody Church when I was a pastor there. Many who heard them expressed a desire to have them in permanent form. However, let me hasten to point out that in these chapters I have taken a somewhat different approach from the original sermons. I wish now I could preach the series again.

I recognize that the Sermon on the Mount has both present and future implications. It is the former that are emphasized here. In the entire series of studies, I have tried to help the believer today realize what it means to reign in life as an heir of the King through Jesus Christ. I believe that God wants each of His children to live like a king and that the Beatitudes help point the way to that experience.

Knowing the imperfections of both the author and the book, I tremble as I send these pages forth. But if they help some believer enter more fully into the privileges of the throne, then I will consider the work rewarded. "Brothers, I do not consider myself yet to have taken hold of it" (Philippians 3:13).

ARE YOU WALKING OR RIDING?

Imagine what it would be like to feature an interview with King Solomon on a TV news show. He was "wiser than any other man" (1 Kings 4:31), the composer of more than a thousand songs, and author of three thousand proverbs. (Imagine the books and CDs he could sell!) He could intelligently discuss trees, animals, birds, insects, and fish, and he was no ignoramus when it came to buildings, horses, money, or (sad to say) idolatrous women. He was a keen observer of the world around him and was able to draw wisdom from events that would appear insignificant to other people.

One day he looked out his window and saw some travelers going by, some walking and some riding horses. He wrote in his journal: "There is an evil I have seen under the sun, the sort of error that arises from a ruler: Fools are put in many high positions, while the rich occupy the low ones. I have seen slaves on horseback, while princes go on foot like slaves" (Ecclesiastes 10:5–7).

Princes are supposed to ride on horses, and their slaves are supposed to walk beside them. But Solomon saw the situation reversed: Those who were supposed to serve were ruling, and those who were supposed to rule were serving. The world was topsy-turvy—and it still is today.

Take, for example, the marvelous machine we call the human body. God made it to be the servant of the spirit, but in the lives of many people it is the master. The appetites ride on horseback while the spirit trudges along on foot. The same reversal exists when it comes to money and material things. God gave them to be our servants, but somehow they have become our masters.

In other words, too many people are walking when they should be riding. Too many people are acting like servants when in fact they are princes, heirs of the King.

God created us to rule as His heirs, and everything else is to be our servant. The fact that we are created in the image of God is proof enough of this statement. But God's words to the first man and woman make our rulership even more exciting: "God blessed them and said to them, 'Be fruitful and increase in number; fill the earth and subdue it. Rule over the fish of the sea and the birds of the air and over every living creature that moves on the ground'"(Genesis 1:28). "Rule over" means "live like a king!" Our first parents were not simply tenants in Paradise; they were the rulers.

"If God created us to be His heirs and live like kings," you may be asking at this point, "then what happened?" Humans certainly don't have dominion over the fish and fowl and animals today. For that matter, they don't even have dominion over themselves."

Good question. What did happen so that people stopped living like kings and started living like servants? When did they get off their horses and start walking? *When they disobeyed God*. When Adam and Eve deliberately disobeyed God's commandment, they went from sovereigns to sinners to servants. They lost their crowns. They got off the horse and started walking, and they became the servants instead of the rulers. And every child of Adam (and that means each one of us) is born a slave.

Can we do anything to change the situation? Yes. For just as God the Father created us, His heirs, to be kings, God the Son redeemed us to be kings. In His death, burial, and resurrection,

Jesus Christ undid all that Adam's sin accomplished—and much more. The dominion that was lost through Adam's disobedience has been regained through Christ's obedience, and there is no longer any need for you and me to be walking like slaves. Romans 5:17 puts it beautifully: "For if, by the trespass of the one man [Adam], death reigned through that one man, how much more will those who receive God's abundant provision of grace and of the gift of righteousness reign in life through the one man, Jesus Christ."

Note those key words: They will "reign in life." Who will reign in life? Those who have received God's free gift of grace and righteousness in Jesus Christ. And it does not say *reign in death* or *reign in future kingdom*. It says *reign in life*. That means we may live like an heir of the King right here and now.

In my ministry I have met many slaves who have become kings by yielding themselves to Jesus Christ. I remember Harry, who, with his wife, stopped at the church study one Friday afternoon. He was a church member, but he was also an alcoholic. Nobody knew it except Harry and his wife and a few close drinking pals. This had been going on for years. Harry would work hard at his job all week and never touch a drop. Then Friday night would arrive, and he would take off for the tavern. He would be "under the influence" all that night and all day Saturday and would sober up in time to be in Sunday school Sunday morning.

"I'm sick of it," he told me. "Tell me what to do."

I told him what to do. "Harry, you've got to turn yourself over to Jesus Christ and let Him be the Lord of your life."

He did it, and the change was immediate. He got back on the horse and started living like a king. And not only that, but he devoted himself to helping others find their true kingship in Jesus Christ. Whenever people having problems with alcohol called on me, I always sent them to Harry, because he could help them better than I could. The last I heard, Harry was still riding on the horse, and his body was his servant instead of his master.

God the Father created you to be a king, God the Son redeemed you to be a king, and God the Spirit can empower you to be a king. We reign in life through the power of the Spirit of God. "For it is God who works in you to will and to act according to his good purpose" (Philippians 2:13). "Now to him who is able to do immeasurably more than all we ask or imagine, according to his power that is at work within us" (Ephesians 3:20). If left to ourselves, we fail; but if we yield to the indwelling Holy Spirit, we succeed. He alone can empower us to live like kings.

The question you must answer is, *Am I walking or riding?* Or, to put it another way, *Am I serving my servants, or are they serving me?* Are you ruling over the appetites of the body? Are you in control of money and material things? (Money is a wonderful servant but a terrible master.) Are you reigning in life?

You can.

This is what the Beatitudes are all about. They explain how you can reign in life and live like an heir of the King. Most people think of the Beatitudes as a collection of idealistic sayings—beautiful to read but impossible to practice. How wrong they are! In fact, the entire Sermon on the Mount is a glorious explanation of what life is really like when you reign through the power of the Holy Spirit. Dr. G. Campbell Morgan called the Sermon on the Mount "The Manifesto of the King," and that is just what it is. Jesus Christ the King is telling us how to live like kings. He is explaining how to reign over such servants as *ego*, so that you practice humility and not pride; *power*, so that you build up and do not destroy; *appetite*, so that you crave purity and not sin. The Beatitudes tell you how to get back in the saddle so that you are riding like a king and not trudging like a slave.

Believe me, you *can* live like a king, provided you know Jesus Christ as your Savior and completely yield to Him. We "reign in life through the one man, Jesus Christ" (Romans 5:17). Jesus Christ is the only king that God will recognize. Jesus was born a king: "Where is the one who has been born king of the Jews?" (Matthew 2:2). He lived as a king in spite of the opposition of wicked people and Satan himself.

Since Adam, Jesus Christ is the only man to walk this earth and exercise the kind of dominion that God originally gave us when He created us. For example, Jesus had dominion over the fish of the sea. He gave Peter a great catch of fish when it seemed impossible to catch anything (Luke 5:1–11); He even brought *one fish* to Peter's hook when the apostle had to pay his temple tax (Matthew 17:24–27). Jesus also had dominion over the fowl of the air. He kept every bird in Jerusalem quiet until the cock was supposed to crow, announcing Peter's denial of Christ. Jesus even had dominion over the beasts of the field. During His temptation, He was in the wilderness "with the wild animals" (Mark 1:13). And He rode into Jerusalem on a colt "which no one [had] ever ridden" (Mark 11:2). Jesus Christ is the last Adam, exercising the dominion lost by the disobedience of the first Adam, and He wants to share that dominion with you and me.

Jesus Christ was born a king, He lived as a king, and He died as a king. True, the only crown He wore was a mocking crown of thorns. And His only throne was a cross bearing the inscription, "This is the King of the Jews." To human eyes, His crucifixion seemed like defeat, but to the King it meant victory. His supreme act of sovereignty was laying down His life for the sins of the world. He was not murdered; He willingly gave His life as your substitute and mine. Never was His kingship more evident than in Gethsemane and at Golgotha, where He "became obedient to death—even death on a cross!" (Philippians 2:8). The greatest test of our kingship is how we use our authority. Jesus used His authority to save others, even though it meant He could not save Himself.

Today Jesus Christ reigns as king, for God "raised him from the dead and seated him at his right hand in the heavenly realms, far above all" (Ephesians 1:20–21). "For he must reign until he has put all his enemies under his feet"(1 Corinthians 15:25).

The tragedy is that too many people echo that rebellious cry of centuries ago: "We don't want this man to be our king" (Luke 19:14). This rebellion is the explanation for the problems in our world today: People believe they are free when in reality they are slaves. "The kings of the earth take their stand and the rulers gather together against the Lord and against his Anointed One. 'Let us break their chains,' they say, 'and throw off their fetters.'" (Psalm 2:2–3). But in rejecting Christ and refusing to submit to God's Word, people are only forfeiting their own kingship. We reign in life by submitting to the authority of God.

George Matheson expressed it perfectly:

> My will is not my own
> Till Thou hast made it Thine;
> If it would reach the monarch's throne,
> It must its crown resign.

God the Father created you to be a king, and you cannot enjoy the fulfillment of your life until you experience this kingship through Jesus Christ. God the Son redeemed you to be a king, but you cannot reign in life until He is your Savior and Lord. God the Spirit can enable you to live like a king, but His power is limited until you yield your all to Him. Your kingship depends on your relationship to God, and your relationship to God depends on the decision of your own will.

"I have seen slaves on horseback, while princes go on foot like slaves."

As a prince, an heir of the King, you were meant to live like a king.

Are you walking or riding?

THE KING IS HERE!

A NEW BOOK

The Beatitudes are part of what we call the Sermon on the Mount, and the Sermon on the Mount is a part of the gospel of Matthew, the gospel of the King. If we are going to understand the message of the Beatitudes, then we are going to have to know something about both the gospel of Matthew and the Sermon on the Mount. Matthew 1:1 is a key verse: "A record of the genealogy of Jesus Christ the son of David, the son of Abraham."

The Old Testament is "the written account of Adam's line" (Genesis 5:1), and, of course, Adam was the first king in human history. God blessed Adam and told him to "rule over the fish of the sea and the birds of the air and over every living creature that moves on the ground" (Genesis 1:28). But those who cannot rule over themselves do not have a right to rule over others. That explains why God tested Adam, for if Adam was to be God's king, he had to be under authority before he could exercise authority.

Adam failed, and his sin plunged the human race into depravity and death. When you read "the written account of Adam's line," you find failure in generation after generation. Abraham lied about his wife, and so did Isaac, his son. Jacob was a schemer, and Moses was a murderer. David was an adulterer and murderer. And these men were the spiritual leaders of the Jewish nation! No wonder the Old Testament ends with the ominous words, "or else I will come and strike the land with a curse" (Malachi 4:6).

What a relief it is to turn to the gospel of Matthew and enter a new book, "the record of the genealogy of Jesus Christ the son of David, the son of Abraham" (Matthew 1:1). Here is God's new king! And unlike the first Adam, Jesus Christ, the "last Adam" (1 Corinthians 15:45), obeyed God and was therefore able to exercise dominion. Because He was under authority, He was able to exercise authority. The first Adam was tested in a beautiful garden and failed, but the last Adam was tested in a dangerous wilderness, and triumphed. Because the first Adam was a thief, he was cast out of Paradise, but the last Adam turned to a thief on a cross and said, "Today you will be with me in paradise" (Luke 23:43). "The written account of Adam's line" ends with a curse, but the "record of the genealogy of Jesus Christ" ends with the promise: "No longer will there be any curse" (Revelation 22:3).

You and I were born the first time into "Adam's line," and that made us sinners and slaves. When you are born again through faith in Jesus Christ, you enter "the genealogy of Jesus Christ," and you are born an heir of God and a king. "To him who loves us and has freed us from our sins by his blood, and has made us to be a kingdom and priests to serve his God and Father" (Revelation 1:5–6). Because we belong to the family of the King, we "reign in life through the one man, Jesus Christ" (Romans 5:17).

The gospel of Matthew presents Jesus Christ as God's king. In the first ten chapters, Matthew answers the three questions most people would ask about a king: Where did He come from? What does He believe? What can He do? In Matthew 1–4, the *person* of the King is presented: His background, birth, baptism, and temptation. In those chapters we are assured that Jesus Christ is the

Son of God, sent by the Father to be the Savior of the world. In Matthew 5–7, the Sermon on the Mount, we have the *principles of* the King: what He believes and what He wants to do in our lives. Chapters 8–10 reveal the *power* of the King and show us our Lord's power over demons, disease, and even death. In other words, in Jesus Christ we have the perfect king. When you trust Him as your Savior, He sets you free from sin and judgment, and He enables you to reign in life as an heir of the King and enjoy His spiritual kingdom here and now.

A NEW KINGDOM

But what kind of a kingdom do we share as we yield to Christ and reign in life? The answer to that question is given in the Sermon on the Mount. It is unfortunate that people rob this magnificent sermon of its importance by claiming that it applies only to the Jews or only to some future period in God's prophetic plan. It is my conviction that the Sermon on the Mount applies to Christians today—and only to Christians. To apply it to unsaved nations is to twist the Scriptures, and to move it into some future age is to rob it of its spiritual power today. I might add that the purpose of the Sermon on the Mount is not evangelism, although certainly the Spirit could use it to give light to a seeking sinner. (I had a Jewish friend who was converted reading the genealogy in Matthew 1, but I do not recommend you add the chapter to your tools for evangelism.) The Sermon on the Mount was given to explain to the disciples the kind of kingdom Jesus wants to build in the lives of His followers.

When our Lord began His ministry, there were several groups in Palestine that claimed to have the answer to Israel's problems. The Pharisees clamed that the nation could experience freedom and blessing only if the people returned to the traditions of the fathers. The Sadducees, on the other hand, urged the people to update their religion and become more liberal. The Essenes taught that salvation would come only through separation from the world, so they established their own communities and remained outside the life of the nation. At the other extreme were Zealots, a revolutionary group that sought to overthrow Rome by revolt and force. Unwilling to wait for gradual change, the Zealots murdered and destroyed in the name of Jewish patriotism.

If you look deeply enough, you will see that we have similar groups today. We have those who cry, "Go back!" and attempt to return us to the "the good old days" of our fathers. Another group cries, "Go ahead!" and urges us to modernize and liberalize our religion and our philosophy of life. The radical extremists shout, "Go against!" and try to destroy vital institutions necessary for the strength and progress of society. The separatists say, "Go out!" and isolate themselves from the very people who may need their help. The names of the groups will change from generation to generation, but the basic aims are the same.

In contrast to all of these solutions to the human problem is what Jesus calls the "kingdom of God" or the "kingdom of heaven." (Matthew seemed to prefer "kingdom of heaven," probably because his Jewish readers would be afraid to pronounce the name of God.) In the Sermon on the Mount, Jesus in effect says, "All of these approaches are right in some respects and wrong in other respects. Their chief weakness is that they are fragmentary; they each deal with a facet of truth but not with the whole of truth."

For example, there is nothing wrong with the tradition of the fathers. But the Old Testament law was temporary; it was preparation for the coming of the Messiah, Jesus Christ. We should not duplicate the religion of Israel under the old covenant. Instead, we must let this Old Testament truth develop into New Testament truth through Jesus Christ. That is why Jesus said, "Do not think that I have come to abolish the Law or the Prophets; I have not come to abolish them but to fulfill them" (Matthew 5:17). The Old Testament law was the seed; the gospel of Christ is the fruit. You can destroy a seed by pulverizing it with a hammer or by planting it in the ground and letting it fulfill its purpose by becoming a plant. It destroys itself by fulfilling itself. This is how Jesus Christ fulfilled the law: He brought it to its fruition in His life, death, and resurrection, and now "the righteous requirements of the law [are] fully met in us, who do not live according to the sinful nature but according to the Spirit" (Romans 8:4).

If the Pharisees wanted to hold on to the past and reject the present, the Sadducees went to the other extreme: They wanted to take the rational approach to life and sacrifice the authority of the Word on the altar of intellectual credibility. They were the modernists of their day. Jesus agreed with them that the Word must be a living reality today, but He rejected their anti-supernatural approach. "The Sadducees say that there is no resurrection, and that there are neither angels nor spirits" (Acts 23:8). When the Sadducees tried to trip Jesus up with their theological questions, He swept them aside with one devastating statement: "You are in error because you do not know the Scriptures or the power of God" (Matthew 22:29). It is through the Word of God and the power of God by His Spirit that believers today experience the reign of God in their lives. The Pharisees lost the present by trying to return to the past. The Sadducees lost the present by denying the past. Both were wrong.

Jesus would have sympathized with the Essenes in their desire for holy living, but He would have rejected their isolationism. If the Sermon on the Mount emphasizes anything, it is that sin is a matter of the heart and not merely outward action. People do not have to murder to be sinners; they only have to hate (Matthew 5:21–26). And they can carry hateful hearts into the desert wastes with them. Years ago, a religious college announced in its catalog: "Our campus is located forty miles from any known sin." What a preposterous claim! The Sermon on the Mount emphasizes holy living, but not at the expense of the normal duties and demands of human life. A change in geography is no guarantee of an improvement in character.

As for the Zealots, Jesus chose one of their number to be one of His disciples: "Simon, who was called the Zealot" (Luke 6:15). Imagine selecting a political fanatic to be among the first disciples! No doubt Jesus admired their zeal and devotion, just as He certainly opposed their violent methods. He would say to Simon, "Yes, some things in 'the establishment' need to be destroyed, but not through hatred, violence, and human force. The weapons we use are not of the flesh; they are of the Spirit. It is not by killing others but by being willing to die yourself that you will establish God's kingdom."

The Sermon on the Mount has for its theme our Lord's statement in Matthew 5:20: "For I tell you that unless your righteousness surpasses that of the Pharisees and the teachers of the law, you will certainly not enter the kingdom of heaven."

A NEW RIGHTEOUSNESS

What was wrong with the righteousness of the scribes and Pharisees? For one thing, they believed that holiness was a matter only of outward actions, and they ignored the inward attitudes of the heart. Their righteousness was only external, a safe system of dos and don'ts by which they could measure their spirituality. In one of His parables, Jesus had the Pharisee pray: "God, I thank you that I am not like other men—robbers, evildoers, adulterers—or even like this tax collector. I fast twice a week and give a tenth of all I get" (Luke 18:11–12). Certainly there is nothing good about being an extortionist or an adulterer, and there is nothing bad about fasting or tithing. But if that is the whole of a person's religion, he or she has nothing. And if people are proud of their religious activities to the point of looking down upon fellow sinners, then they are in bad condition spiritually.

In the Beatitudes Jesus teaches us that true righteousness is a matter of the heart. It has been well said: "The Beatitudes describe the *attitudes* that ought to *be* in the believer's life." What good are tithing, fasting, and outward obedience to rules and regulations if the heart is proud, critical, and condemning? Conduct must be based upon character. "Man looks at the outward appearance, but the Lord looks at the heart" (1 Samuel 16:7). "Above all else, guard your heart, for it is the wellspring of life" (Proverbs 4:23).

In Matthew 5:21–48 Jesus illustrates this basic principle that righteousness must be a matter of the heart. He takes some of the traditions of the elders and shows they are inadequate. "You shall not murder" involves much more than physical violence; hatred in the heart is the equivalent of murder with the hand. "You shall not commit adultery" involves much more than an immoral act. Cultivating the desire in the heart is the equivalent of adultery. The Sermon on the Mount goes much deeper than the Ten Commandments, for, with one exception ("You shall not covet"), the Ten Commandments deal only with outward actions, whereas the Sermon on the Mount deals with inward attitudes. In the Sermon on the Mount, Jesus not only breaks away the shell of pharisaic tradition that covered God's law, but He also penetrates to the heart of that law and explains its deeper, spiritual meaning. The Word of God is like seed. The Pharisees put a "crust" of tradition around the seed so that it could not give life and bear fruit. Jesus breaks that crust and then opens the husk of the seed so the spiritual life can be fulfilled in us.

The Beatitudes, then, are a description of true righteousness in contrast to the false righteousness of the scribes and Pharisees. If we are going to live like heirs of the King, then we must manifest this kind of character; and we can do it only through the power of the Holy Spirit. Interestingly enough, the Holy Spirit is not even mentioned in these chapters, yet it is obvious that believers could never in their own power attain this high level of Christian experience. "For what the law was powerless to do in that it was weakened by the sinful nature, God did by sending his own Son in the likeness of sinful man to be a sin offering. And so he condemned sin in sinful man, in order that the righteous requirements of the law might be fully met in us, who do not live according to the sinful nature but according to the Spirit" (Romans 8:3–4).

Not only were the Pharisees and scribes mistaken about righteousness and sin, but they were also mistaken in their motives for serving God, and Jesus deals with this error in Matthew 6. The Pharisees and scribes were religious in order to get the approval and praise of others. But true Christians have a greater motive than that: They live for the approval and praise of God. After all, if true righteousness is a matter of the heart and only God can see the heart, then only God can give the reward. "I am he who searches hearts and minds" (Revelation 2:23). Jesus warns us in Matthew 6 not to "do righteousness"—whether it be giving, fasting, or praying—in order to be seen of others. He says, "Live your life before the eye of God, not the eyes of others. Your Father sees in secret, and that is sufficient. If you live for the praise of others, you have your reward."

The Beatitudes, then, are God's description of Christian character, the kind of character that leads to right conduct. When the Pharisee wondered because Jesus did not go through the ceremonial washing of hands at dinner, Jesus said to him: "Now then, you Pharisees clean the outside of the cup and dish, but inside you are full of greed and wickedness. You foolish people! Did not the one who made the outside make the inside also? But give what is inside the dish to the poor, and everything will be clean for you" (Luke 11:39–41). If there is dirty water coming out of the faucet, I do not buy a new faucet—I cleanse the cistern.

A NEW CHALLENGE

In this book we will consider the Beatitudes individually, but there is truth to be gained by first considering them collectively. To begin with, the Beatitudes show us how to enter the kingdom. The first step is admitting my spiritual bankruptcy and having a humble, honest attitude toward myself. "Blessed are the poor in spirit" applies the ax to the very root of pharisaical pride and hypocrisy. "Blessed are they that mourn" deals with my attitude toward my sin; instead of criticizing the other person, I judge myself. "Blessed are the meek" deals with my attitude toward God: I am submissive to Him and not trying to impress Him with who I am or what I have done. When I "hunger and thirst after righteousness," then God provides that righteousness in the person of His Son, Jesus Christ. Like the Pharisee Saul of Tarsus, I exchange my own self-righteousness for the grace-righteousness of Christ (Philippians 3:1–11).

But this is more than a commercial transaction, for the results can be seen in everyday life. Having received the righteousness of Christ, I can begin to manifest in my life the character of God.

I become merciful instead of condemning; I seek to cultivate purity of heart; I become a peacemaker, not a troublemaker. As I grow to become more like Christ, I experience the kind of treatment He received when He was on earth—reviling, persecution, and false accusations. But because of His grace, I become salt and light in a world that is decayed and dark. Having entered the kingdom, it is now my privilege to enlarge the kingdom by applying His righteousness in the world about me.

This means that the Beatitudes are practically meaningless to the person who has never trusted Jesus Christ as Savior. They may illustrate an ideal, but that ideal can never be reached in human strength alone. But the person who begins with "blessed are the poor in spirit" should ultimately come to that place of trusting the Savior. "This is the one I esteem," says the Lord, "he who is humble and contrite in spirit, and trembles at my word" (Isaiah 66:2).

The Beatitudes tell us how to enter and enlarge the kingdom, but they also tell us how to enjoy the kingdom. "Blessed are . . . for they will . . ." They will *what*? Just read the promises, and you will see how much believers enjoy from God when they seek to cultivate true Christian character. "Theirs is the kingdom"—authority. "They will be comforted"—encouragement. "They will inherit the earth"—provision for every need. "They will be filled"—satisfaction. "They will be shown mercy"—provision for ministry to others. "They will see God"—spiritual vision. "They will be called sons of God"—becoming more like God in daily life. There is a price to pay, but the results are well worth it.

Jesus Christ invites you and me into a life of enrichment and enlargement.

Will you and I pay the price?

Blessed are the poor in spirit,
for theirs is the kingdom of heaven.
(MATTHEW 5:3)

●

Unless you change and become like little children,
you will never enter the kingdom of heaven.
(MATTHEW 18:3)

●

Everyone who exalts himself will be humbled,
and he who humbles himself will be exalted.
(LUKE 18:14)

●

Humble yourselves, therefore, under God's mighty hand,
that he may lift you up in due time.
(1 PETER 5:6)

●

God opposes the proud but gives grace to the humble.
(JAMES 4:6)

3

THE POOR IN SPIRIT

CONFUSION

What does it mean to be poor in spirit?

Most assuredly, it does not mean being poor-spirited. Unfortunately, there are some people who have little or no self-esteem and whose self-image is poor; as a consequence, their inner person is anemic.

I once counseled a young man who, during childhood, had heard nothing from his father but, "You are good for nothing and will never amount to anything!" The young man had such a low opinion of himself that he failed in everything he attempted, and every failure only added to his emotional and spiritual bankruptcy. I pointed out to him that he was important to God and therefore ought to have more self-esteem. After all, he was created in the image of God. Even more, Jesus Christ died for him and the Holy Spirit lived in him, so he was worth something. All of this theology he accepted with his mind, but down in his heart he could still hear his father telling him how worthless he was.

Some people are shy and retiring by nature, but that is not the same as being poor in spirit. God created us with different temperaments and personalities; some of us are extroverts, whereas others are introverts. But it is possible to be an introvert and proud or an extrovert and humble. Peter was certainly an extrovert, yet Thomas's refusal to accept the fact of Christ's resurrection—and his demand for proof—was just as much an evidence of pride as Peter's boasting and poor swordsmanship. Shyness is not poverty of spirit.

Neither is the detestable, groveling attitude that we call mock humility. The classic example is Uriah Heep in *David Copperfield*, who was always reminding people that he was "but a very 'umble person." In a more refined way, we see this mock humility in the people who deny about themselves what everybody else knows is true. I once worked with a Sunday school teacher who had a great gift of working with children, yet she would deny it every time it was mentioned. "Oh, I can't do anything!" she would protest. "I just struggle along until somebody comes to do the job the way it ought to be done!" All of us in the meetings would smile at each other and change the subject. We knew that her "protesting too much" was a veiled request for praise, and none of us felt like praising her.

In a sense Moses was guilty of this sin when he told God he was not able to speak (Exodus 4:10–17). Who can tell God anything about himself that God does not already know? And, after all, God made us, and God is able to empower us to do whatever He calls us to do. Denying that we can accomplish God's work is not humility; it is the worst kind of pride.

Being poor in spirit means knowing yourself, accepting yourself, and being yourself to the glory of God.

It means *knowing* yourself—your strengths and weaknesses, your hidden desires, your ambitions, your spiritual gifts and natural abilities—and being honest with yourself. When I was in grade school, I almost developed an emotional disorder over sports. Both of my older brothers were capable athletes, but I am not, and every time the boys in my class chose sides, I was the last one chosen. At first it was a painful experience. After all, many school children dream of being a great sports star. Then it got to be a joke, and finally I was able to accept the fact that I would never be a great athlete—or even a good player. One of my coaches was sure he could make a trackman out of me, but after I knocked down six hurdles and broke a bone in my foot, he changed his mind. Sometimes getting to know yourself can be a painful experience, but it is a part of maturing.

It also means *accepting* yourself. Some people, when they discover what they really are, deny their discovery and move into a life of pretending. In fact, some people have pretended their way right into a dream world of psychological problems and have completely lost touch with reality. Most of us do not go that far, but the inability to accept yourself can have serious emotional and spiritual consequences. When you accept yourself, you find it easier to accept others and also easier to accept God's plan for your life. It did not take me long to accept the fact that I was neither an athlete nor a mechanic. (I handle a hammer about as well as I do a baseball bat.) But early in grade school I discovered a flair for words, and I have been speaking them and writing them ever since.

Being poor in spirit means knowing yourself, accepting yourself, and *being* yourself to the glory of God—your best self, of course, and not anything less. That means constant growing in every area of your life. It means using your strengths to overcome your weaknesses and using your weaknesses to discover the mighty power of God. "When I am weak, then I am strong" (2 Corinthians 12:10). Being yourself involves yielding to the Spirit of God and permitting Him to fulfill God's will in your life. You are not imitating somebody else or envying somebody else. You are yourself—your best self—empowered by the Spirit of God to do what God has called you to do.

To be poor in spirit means knowing that in myself I am bankrupt, but in Christ I am rich. It means discovering the place God wants me to fill and filling it for His glory, no matter how insignificant or unimportant I may believe it is. The person who is truly poor in spirit knows that *every* place of God's choosing is an important place. "The eye cannot say to the hand, 'I don't need you!' And the head cannot say to the feet, 'I don't need you'" (1 Corinthians 12:21). The believer who is poor in spirit is in the place of God's choosing, fulfilling the purpose of God's choosing and depending on the power that God alone can supply.

Perhaps the word *humility* is another way of saying "poor in spirit." I believe it was Andrew Murray who said that humility is that grace that, when you know you have it, you have lost it. He also said, "Humility is not thinking meanly of yourself. It is simply not thinking of yourself at all!" This explains why "blessed are the poor in spirit" is the first of the Beatitudes, for until we admit our need we can never receive what God has for us. Too many people are like those in the Laodicean church; they are "rich . . . have acquired wealth and do not need a thing" (Revelation 3:17). And, like the Laodiceans, they don't know that they are "wretched, pitiful, poor, blind and naked."

To be poor in spirit does not mean to deny your personality or try to suppress it. It simply means yielding it to God for Him to make it all that He wants it to be. The motto is old but true: "God always gives His best to those who leave the choice with Him."

CHARACTERISTICS

There are several evidences of humility in the life of the believer. To begin with, when you are poor in spirit, you *accept others, because you have accepted yourself*. That does not mean you always agree with what they are or what they do, but you accept them just the same. When others succeed you are happy for them; when they fail you try to encourage them. If I find myself happy when they fail and sad when they succeed, then I am not poor in spirit. I am proud. When young David killed Goliath, King Saul was glad to get rid of his enemy and honor David, but when David started slaying his ten thousands in contrast to Saul's thousands, then the king became envious and angry. David was poor in spirit: "Who am I, and what is my family or my father's clan in Israel, that I should become the king's son-in-law?" (1 Samuel 18:18). At no time did David use his position to promote himself; he was willing for God to do the promoting in His time and in His way. "In everything he did he had great success, because the Lord was with him" (1 Samuel 18:14).

A constant source of friction among the disciples—and it must have grieved their Master's heart—was, "Who is the greatest in the kingdom of heaven?" (Matthew 18:1). Our Lord's answer was to place an unspoiled child in their midst. Why are unspoiled children great, so much so that people will risk their lives to protect and save them? They are great because they know they are children and act like children. There is something unsettling and distasteful about children who act like adults and expect to be treated as one. (Perhaps the only thing worse is an adult acting like a child.) But when children naturally act like children, they are beautiful to behold and loveable. Children without guile or affectation are sovereigns; the entire world bows before their little throne!

King Saul could not become like a little child and, as a result, lost his crown, his kingdom, and his life. He pretended to be something that he was not. Samuel commanded him to wait for the prophet's arrival before any sacrifices were offered, but Saul could not wait. He pretended to be a priest (1 Samuel 13:5–14), and he impetuously offered the sacrifice. Later, when God gave him another chance and commanded him to exterminate the Amalekites, Saul pretended to be God and deliberately disobeyed the orders (1 Samuel 15). The final scene in Saul's life shows the king completely abandoned by God (1 Samuel 28). He prayed but received no answers; even the dreams, the priests, and the prophets brought no message from God. So he decided to consult a witch. "Saul disguised himself," 1 Samuel 28:8 says, and went by night to a witch's cave. In one sense Saul did disguise himself, but in another sense he was revealing his true self. All along he had been rebelling against God, and "rebellion is like the sin of divination" (1 Samuel 15:23). The next day Saul committed suicide on the field of battle, and a man who claimed to be an Amalekite—one of the men Saul himself should have slain—took his crown (2 Samuel 1:10).

Another evidence of poverty of spirit is *accepting circumstances*. When circumstances do not go my way, do I become angry and critical? Am I always trying to manipulate people and circumstances for my own benefit and comfort? Or am I willing to give in to make things easier for somebody else? Do I cut corners and pull deals to accomplish what I want in life? Paul said, "I have learned to be content whatever the circumstances" (Philippians 4:11). That does not mean that Christians never try to improve their circumstances, because that would be complacency, not contentment. But it does mean that the poor in spirit do not chafe in uncomfortable circumstances and spend their time complaining both to God and others.

A third evidence is *a right attitude toward things*. Those who are poor in spirit do not find their satisfaction in things; they can do with or without. "I know what it is to be in need, and I know what it is to have plenty" (Philippians 4:12). People who are poor in spirit do not measure a man's worth by his material wealth, for "a man's life does not consist in the abundance of his possessions" (Luke 12:15). If things change my attitudes, then things are my master—not my servant—and that is the sin of idolatry. The proud person is possessed by things; the humble person possesses things and uses them for the good of others and the glory of God.

The parable of the rich farmer illustrates this truth (Luke 12:13–21). Material wealth is either a window through which we see God or a mirror in which we see ourselves, and with this farmer it was the latter. There are eleven personal pronouns in this farmer's conversation with himself. He talks *about* himself *to* himself. And he had no thought for God or his hungry neighbor. Had he been poor in spirit he would have been rich toward God, but because he believed he was rich, he became poor and lost everything. He believed he was an owner, but he discovered (too late) that he was only a steward. God was the owner, and all the fruits and goods were merely on loan. The farmer possessed, but he did not own.

Thoreau was correct when he wrote, "A man is rich in proportion to the number of things which he can afford to let alone." Paul expressed it even better: "For we brought nothing into the world, and we can take nothing out of it. But if we have food and clothing, we will be content with that" (1 Timothy 6:7–8). Those who are poor in spirit do not build their lives on things. They have God, and that is all they need.

Let me suggest a fourth evidence of humility: *accepting God's will for your life*. The person who is poor in spirit joyfully accepts the will of God; the proud person resists God's will. I have met people who are so proud that they even defy God. I remember a Christian couple that had big plans for their children and told God what He was supposed to do. He did it, and they lived to regret it. "So he gave them what they asked for, but sent a wasting disease upon them" (Psalm 106:15).

Sometimes God gives us seeming failure to teach us to submit to His will. I learned that lesson in a little fishing village in Denmark, where I ministered with a Youth for Christ team in 1957. I did not know the language, the people of the village did not seem interested in the gospel, and I felt like quitting. Few people were attending the services, but night after night my associate and I led the singing and preached the Word. Before the week ended, we learned that God had indeed changed some hearts. During that week I learned to obey God's will in spite of my feelings and in spite of the results, a lesson I hope I never forget.

The person who is self-satisfied and self-sufficient, who feels no need for God, is not poor in spirit. The believer who argues with God's will and complains about circumstances is not poor in spirit. The person who fishes for compliments and inflates when compliments come is not poor in spirit. Leaders who are harder on others than they are on themselves are not poor in spirit.

To be poor in spirit, then, means to know yourself, accept yourself, and be yourself to the glory of God. It means letting God use both your strengths and your weaknesses to accomplish His will and glorify His name.

CONSEQUENCES

Why does being poor in spirit bring blessing? An attitude of humility is exactly opposite to what the world teaches and usually opposite to what most people practice. "Assert yourself!" is the world's slogan. But Jesus says, "Humble yourself." How can humility bring blessing to you when you live in a cutthroat world?

To begin with, humility is godlike, and anything that makes us more like God is bound to bring blessing, even if the world will not accept it. "Who is like the Lord our God, the One who sits enthroned on high, who stoops down [humbles himself] to look on the heavens and the earth?" (Psalm 113:5–6). God the Father humbles Himself to behold the things both in heaven and on earth. God the Son "humbled himself and became obedient to death—even death on a cross!" (Philippians 2:8). Think of the humility of the Holy Spirit as He lives with us day by day!

It is difficult to conceive of a Christian growing in grace apart from humility. True poverty of spirit is the soil out of which the fruit of the Spirit can be cultivated. "This is the one I esteem: he who is humble and contrite in spirit, and trembles at my word" (Isaiah 66:2). Certainly the seed of God's Word could never be planted in the hard soil of a proud heart. "Break up your unplowed ground and do not sow among thorns" (Jeremiah 4:3).

But there is another reason poverty of spirit brings blessing: It makes us kings. "Blessed are the poor in spirit: for theirs is the kingdom of heaven." We control by being controlled. No person has a right to exercise authority who himself or herself is not under authority. We reign in life by submitting to the authority of Jesus Christ (Romans 5:17).

What is involved in reigning in life? It means authority, for when we submit to Christ, He is able to share His authority with us. Pride always weakens us because pride cuts us off from fellowship with the Lord. Peter was his weakest when, in pride, he wielded his sword and tried to defend Jesus. Peter was his strongest when he wept bitterly, humbled himself, and submitted to Jesus. Jesus used a little child as the perfect example of a citizen of His kingdom because in a child you see authority based on humility. Because children are so weak in themselves, they command all the strength of those about them. The world believes that authority comes from size, ability, noise, and self-promotion; the Christian knows that true authority comes from poverty of spirit. We reign as kings because we submit as servants.

This spiritual kingdom involves not only authority but also liberty. Pride always makes a slave of a person, whereas humility sets that person free. When you live to promote yourself, you are bound to become a slave of people or things or circumstances. You are never really free to be yourself, because self has already enslaved you through pride. Those who are poor in spirit are not disturbed by the attitudes or criticisms of others because they live to please God. Moses was not afraid of Pharaoh because Pharaoh could do nothing to hurt God's servant so long as that servant was submitted to the Lord. When you live to promote yourself, you must always get something from others to inflate your ego or advertise your importance; but every time you receive something you pay dearly. "Please honor me before the elders of my people and before Israel" pleaded King Saul (1 Samuel 15:30). His pride made him a slave. He was not the king of Israel: Israel was king over him.

Humility means that you look to God for everything you need. This sets you free from people, circumstances, and things. If you need nothing but God, then nothing—and no one—can be a threat to you. You are free.

Humility makes us kings, not only by giving us authority and liberty but also by giving us adequacy. "The Lord brings death and makes alive; he brings down to the grave and raises up. The Lord sends poverty and wealth; he humbles and he exalts. He raises the poor from the dust and lifts the needy from the ash heap; he seats them with princes and has them inherit a throne of honor (1 Samuel 2:6–8). When we are low enough, then God can trust us with a throne and a scepter. He opens the treasures of His grace to the dead, the poor, and the beggars. His feast is spread for "the poor, the crippled, the blind and the lame" (Luke 14:21), not the proud who believe their souls can be satisfied with lands, oxen, and honeymoons.

There is poverty in riches, and there are riches in poverty. "One man . . . pretends to be poor, yet has great wealth" (Proverbs 13:7). "For you know the grace of our Lord Jesus Christ, that though he was rich, yet for your sakes he became poor, so that you through his poverty might become rich" (2 Corinthians 8:9). People who depend on material things cannot reign in life because they are possessed by the things they possess. Things control them, and they are never satisfied with the things that they have.

When you and I are poor in spirit, God gives us a kingdom, and we reign in life as His heirs. When King Saul was a humble servant, God gave him a kingdom, but when Saul began to throw his weight around and run things his own way, then he lost his kingdom. How did David get his kingdom? By being a nobody. This is how Jesus Christ secured His kingdom: "Therefore God exalted him to the highest place and gave him the name that is above every name" (Philippians 2:9). This is the paradox of the Christian life: We surrender that we might reign. This leads to authority, liberty, and adequacy.

CULTIVATION

How can we cultivate this grace of humility? How is it possible to succeed in this difficult world while seeking to be poor in spirit?

I believe the first step is to *accept God's estimate of yourself*. You had to do this to become a Christian, and you have to do this to grow in the Christian life. When Christ first confronted you with the gospel, you perhaps had a difficult time agreeing with His estimate of your life. "For all have sinned and fall short of the glory of

God" (Romans 3:23). "There is no one righteous, not even one" (Romans 3:10). "You must be born again" (John 3:7). Once you accepted God's estimate of yourself, it was easy to accept God's remedy for your sins. You had to humble yourself, and then God lifted you up.

"For by the grace given me I say to every one of you: Do not think of yourself more highly than you ought, but rather think of yourself with sober judgment, in accordance with the measure of faith God has given you" (Romans 12:3). Paul is not suggesting that we not think of ourselves, because that would be impossible. He is warning us not to think *more highly* of ourselves than we ought to; and I believe we ought to include *less* highly as well. There is a false humility that degrades as much as does a proud spirit. I suggested early in this chapter that true humility means knowing myself, accepting myself, and being myself to the glory of God. This means accepting God's estimate of me on the basis of the gifts and the faith He has given me.

For example, Moses argued with God when God called him to go to Egypt (Exodus 3–4). Moses used every excuse he could find, all of them centered on his own weaknesses. Gideon made the same mistake when God called him to deliver the people from the power of Midian. Imagine God calling a fearful farmer a "mighty warrior" (Judges 6:12)! Imagine Jesus Christ calling Simon a "rock" (Matthew 16:18)! When Moses, Gideon, and Simon accepted God's estimate and acted upon it by faith, they accomplished great things for God. They found their kingdom by humbly yielding to God and daring to believe what He said. Every victory they won was the result of their faith in God's Word.

As you read your Bible, notice what God says about you as a child of God. Accept what He says and act upon it. When Moses, Gideon, and Simon argued with the Word of God, it led to defeat.

When they accepted the Word and acted upon it, the result was victory. God does not say to us, "Obey, and I will bless you." Rather, He in effect says, "I have already blessed you with all spiritual blessings in Christ; now, draw upon this wealth, believe what I say, and live like a king!" (See Ephesians 1:3).

The second step is to *yield yourself to God daily* and draw your strength from Him. "Apart from me you can do nothing" (John 15:5). Many Christians find it helpful to get up early enough in the morning to spend uninterrupted time in prayer and meditation on God's Word. What digestion is to your body, meditation is to your soul, and what food is to digestion, the Word of God is to meditation. "Man does not live on bread alone, but on every word that comes from the mouth of God" (Matthew 4:4). The Word of God taken into your inner person releases power. The Bible is the scepter by which you reign in life. Spend time daily in quiet communion with God and carry the power of that experience with you all through the day. We do not read that King Saul was a great man of prayer or that he meditated on the Word, but in the Psalms we constantly meet King David talking to God and listening as God talked to him.

The Word of God will transform your mind (Romans 12:2) so that you will have "the mind of Christ," the same attitude Jesus had when He laid aside His glory and came to earth as a servant (Philippians 2:5–7). You were not born with the attitude of a servant; you were born with the attitude of a rebel. It is only as the Word transforms the mind that we can ever cultivate true humility and poverty of spirit.

The third step is this: *Focus on Christ and His blessings.* Too many people believe humility comes from studying their own sins and failures, but that is not true. It is not the badness of people that leads to repentance but "the goodness of God" (Romans 2:4 KJV).

If you conduct too many "spiritual autopsies," you may bleed to death. There is nothing wrong with honest self-examination, *provided that you look to Christ.* However, too many Christians spend too much time looking into the mirror when they ought to be "fix[ing their] eyes on Jesus, the author and perfecter of [their] faith" (Hebrews 12:2). The more you contemplate the goodness of God, the lower you will sink before Him. "Who am I, O Lord God, and what is my family, that you have brought me this far?" prayed King David (1 Chronicles 17:16).

Peter's experience with the Lord in Luke 5 is a good illustration of the truth that humility comes from contemplating God's blessings and not our own failures. Peter had fished all night and caught nothing when Jesus entered his boat and used it for a platform as He taught the multitudes. Peter was a captive audience and had to listen to the Word, but this Word was preparing him for a miracle. ("Faith comes from hearing the message, and the message is heard through the word of Christ" [Romans 10:17].) When Jesus commanded Peter to launch out into the deep, the fisherman protested weakly but obeyed, and the result was a great catch of fish. "When Simon Peter saw this, he fell at Jesus' knees and said, 'Go away from me, Lord; I am a sinful man!'" (Luke 5:8). It was not his night of failure that drove Peter to his knees but the great success that Jesus gave to him. Anybody can say, "I am sinful" when he or she has failed, but it takes an honest, humble heart to say this when he or she has succeeded. It was the goodness of God that led Peter to repentance, and if you and I will only meditate on His goodness, we, too, will grow in humility and poverty of spirit.

Next comes the fourth step: *Look for opportunities to serve others.* Humility and service go together. The proud look for others to serve them, whereas the humble look for ways to serve others. "Consider others better than yourselves" (Philippians 2:3). "Serve one another in love" (Galatians 5:13). "But even if I am being poured out like a drink offering on the sacrifice and service coming from your faith, I am glad and rejoice with all of you" (Philippians 2:17). Sacrifice and service are the twin children of humility. It is important to note that this sacrifice and service must often go unnoticed and unrewarded. "They have their reward!" If we blow a trumpet every time we help somebody, we will only nourish our pride and starve our humility. A cup of cold water for Jesus' sake is all that He asks.

Do not look for big opportunities "worthy" of your abilities. Those will come in due time. The great saints of the Bible started as servants, not rulers, and they were faithful over a few things before God made them kings. Moses tended sheep; Joseph was a steward; David was a shepherd; Jesus was a carpenter. Live with the eye of God upon you and forget the praise of others. Serve faithfully in the hidden place, and in due time God will lift you up. Every opportunity for service is an opportunity to exercise sovereignty in Christ. We reign in life by living to serve, to the glory of God.

The sin of pride has ruined more lives than perhaps any other sin. It is the sin that invites Satan to rule. It is the sin that cost King Saul his character, his crown, and, ultimately, his life. Humility is the grace that made David a king.

"Blessed are the poor in spirit: for theirs is the kingdom of heaven."

Blessed are those who mourn, for they will be comforted.
(MATTHEW 5:4)

Godly sorrow brings repentance that leads to salvation
and leaves no regret, but worldly sorrow brings death.
(2 CORINTHIANS 7:10)

And [Peter] went outside and wept bitterly.
(LUKE 22:62)

So Judas threw the money into the temple and left.
Then he went away and hanged himself.
(MATTHEW 27:5)

Sorrowful, yet always rejoicing.
(2 CORINTHIANS 6:10)

He has sent me to bind up the brokenhearted, . . .
to comfort all who mourn.
(ISAIAH 61:1–2)

Weeping may remain for a night,
but rejoicing comes in the morning.
(PSALM 30:5)

4

THE MOURNERS

If you want to know a person's character, find out what makes him or her laugh and weep. This test is not infallible because we all have our difficult days, but generally speaking, it is true. It always amazes me when people laugh at a drunk or at a comedian impersonating a drunk. I see nothing funny in drunkenness or in drunken behavior. As a pastor I have seen too much of the tragedy of drink to be entertained by a drunk.

What we laugh at and weep over indicate our values of life, and values are a part of maturity. Little children will laugh at things that seem stupid to adults, and they will cry over matters that seem trivial to adults. I read about a terrible train accident in Great Britain that killed a number of passengers. In one of the cars was a mother with a little child in her arms, and the mother was dead but the child was unharmed. When the rescuers took the child away from the dead mother, the child laughed and played, but when they took away the child's candy, she broke into a terrible tantrum of weeping and screaming. The fact that her mother was dead did not bother the child because she knew nothing about death. But she did know about candy!

That means that the higher you go in life, the more vulnerable you are in sorrow. You can escape sorrow if you wish to simply by isolating yourself from other people and from the affairs of life, but at the same time you will also be escaping joy. For the higher you go on the scale of life, the greater the opportunities for joy, and the same things that cause joy can also cause sorrow. Animals feel pain, and some pets seem to show sorrow, but for the most part animals know nothing of a broken heart. But how many of us are willing to become animals merely to avoid sorrow? Most children know nothing of the deep hurts that bring tears to adult eyes, but how many of us would want to become children to escape the pains of adult life?

Whenever you enter into the presence of joy, you make yourself a candidate for sorrow. A young couple that marries experiences joy. But suppose she comes down with a terminal illness, or suppose he is hopelessly crippled in an accident? A couple can bring children into the world, and children are a joy. But suppose one of them develops a fatal disease? Just about everything in life that brings joy can also be a source of sorrow, and the wrong way to escape that sorrow is to run away from life.

Jesus never tried to escape the sorrows of life. Neither did He deny that they existed. *He transformed them.* Jesus did not tell His disciples to go out and look for sorrow, but He did tell them that He was able to transform their tears and bring them comfort. Of itself, sorrow never makes a person better. I have seen it make people bitter. But sorrow plus Jesus Christ can bring a transforming experience of power into the life of the one who is mourning.

If you and I are to experience the comfort of God, we must understand the three kinds of sorrow that can come to us in life.

NATURAL SORROW

First, there is *natural* sorrow. This kind of sorrow comes to everybody—saved and unsaved, rich and poor, young and old. It is a natural part of life. God made us to be able to weep. Some of the songs and sermons you hear give the impression that a Christian never weeps. But Abraham, the great man of faith, wept when his dear wife died. David wept when his rebellious son was killed in battle. Jeremiah wept when he saw his beloved nation go into captivity. Jesus wept over the lost city of Jerusalem; He also wept at the tomb of His friend Lazarus. Jesus never wept for Himself, and He admonished the women of Jerusalem not to weep over Him. When Paul said farewell to his dear friends from Ephesus, he wept and they wept. As you read the Bible, you get the impression that God expects His people to weep. "There is a time for everything, and a season for every activity under heaven: a time to be born and a time to die . . . a time to weep and a time to laugh" (Ecclesiastes 3:1–2, 4).

When God created the first man, He gave him the ability to weep, and He did this *before* man had sinned. Natural weeping is not sinful. On the contrary, it is a gift from God. There is healing in natural weeping. Doctors and psychologists have helped us to understand what really happens when we mourn, and their discoveries have helped us (with God's assistance) to heal the brokenhearted. Natural sorrow expressed in mourning releases a healing process in people's lives that enables them to accept the pain, work their way through it, and adjust to life again. In my ministry I have noticed that the people who, for one reason or another, do not mourn, do not easily adjust to new circumstances; their wounds never seem to heal.

Mourning is an expression of love. It is also a proof that the person has accepted the fact of the crisis and wants to handle it in an adult manner. When the pain is kept inside, it poisons the emotional system in the same way an infection spreads through the bloodstream. I have heard well-meaning people say in funeral homes, "Now, don't cry! You know she is better off!" It is wrong to advise people not to cry when the thing they need to do more than anything else is to cry. This is God's way of helping the mourner release the pressure and pain inside, and it is a perfectly natural thing. Some people have the idea that weeping is a sign of weakness. Self-pity is a sign of weakness, but not weeping. Jesus was the strongest man who ever walked on this earth, and He wept openly.

There is a hopeless sorrow that people who do not know Christ experience. "Brothers, we do not want you to be ignorant about those who fall asleep, or to grieve like the rest of men, who have no hope" (1 Thessalonians 4:13). Paul goes on to explain why Christians have hope even while they are weeping. To begin with, for the Christian, death is sleep; the body goes to sleep, and the soul goes home to God. One day Christ will return and bring with Him those who have died in Christ and gone on before us, and we shall "ever be with the Lord" (v. 17). When a Christian loved one or friend dies and we weep, our mourning is certainly not for the loved one but for ourselves. Death is like an amputation, and the closer we are in life the harder it is in death. But our sorrow need not be hopeless because we have eternal hope in Jesus Christ and in the promises of His Word.

UNNATURAL SORROW

The second kind of sorrow is *unnatural* sorrow. It is unnatural because its effects on our lives are opposite to what God wants us to experience. Godly sorrow heals, but unnatural sorrow makes the wounds deeper and fills the heart with pain. Natural sorrow gradually helps us to put life back together again, but unnatural sorrow tears things apart and keeps them that way. When you sorrow in a natural way, you learn to face and accept reality, but unnatural sorrow isolates you from reality and makes it difficult for you to adjust to the demands of life. I have known people who have grieved themselves into physical affliction and even mental unbalance. True sorrow enables us to experience the comfort of God, but unnatural sorrow blinds us to God's comfort and seems to give us, instead, the condemnation of God; there is a growing feeling of guilt instead of an experience of grace. Natural sorrow enables us to remember what has been lost and use those memories constructively; but unnatural sorrow turns memories into punishments that destroy the peace and balance that God wants us to have.

Psychologists who have studied bereavement tell us that unnatural sorrow can have many causes. One major cause is selfishness. Self-centered people use other people—even the closest loved ones—to make their own lives safe and pleasant; if they lose a loved one it upsets their lifestyle, and it hurts. Their tears are more for themselves than for the deceased. Fear is another cause of unnatural sorrow—fear of the future, fear of change, perhaps even fear of death itself. Excessive tears and mourning then become an invisible armor to protect the bereaved from the hard knocks of life. They are saying, "Don't lay any responsibility on me! Don't demand too much of me! Can't you see I have enough to bear already?"

But perhaps the greatest cause of unnatural grief is guilt. It is our way of atoning for past failures and sins in connection with the deceased. Some people atone for their sins by purchasing expensive, elaborate funerals. I recall one lady who took her life's savings—all that she had—and bought her husband the most expensive casket available. She put her financial future into the grave with him, but it was her way of saying to him, "Dear, I'm sorry for the mean things I said and did while you were sick." I think of another man who visited his wife's grave almost every day for months after her death, no matter what the weather was, not as a sign of love but as a work of atonement. It reminded me of the great Samuel Johnson, who stood in the rain with his head uncovered to atone for a boyish act of disobedience to his father.

King David illustrates this unnatural sorrow that results from guilt. You will recall that David's disobedient son, Absalom, tried to take the kingdom away from him—and almost succeeded. We get the impression that Absalom was a favored, pampered son; certainly he was a vain fellow who was proud of his beauty, especially his hair (2 Samuel 14:25–26). He secretly plotted against his father, drove David from Jerusalem, took over the palace, and then planned to attack David's divided forces and utterly wipe them out. Instead, David won the battle and Absalom was slain, a judgment the young man certainly deserved. Before the battle, David begged his leaders, "Deal gently for my sake with the young man, even with Absalom" (2 Samuel 18:5 KJV). When David received the tragic news that Absalom had been slain, he expressed his sorrow in words that have become familiar: "O my son Absalom! My son, my son Absalom! If only I had died instead of you—O Absalom, my son, my son!" (2 Samuel 18:33). While we admire David's love, we question his thinking. Would it have been better for the nation for David to die and for rebellious Absalom to live?

There is no doubt that Absalom's death was part of the payment that David made because of his adultery with Bathsheba. When confronted with the sin of "the rich man" who stole the ewe lamb—a picture of David himself—the king said, "As surely as the Lord lives, the man who did this deserves to die! He must pay for that lamb four times over, because he did such a thing and had no pity" (2 Samuel 12:3–6). David did restore fourfold: the baby died, his daughter Tamar was violated, his son Amnon was slain, and Absalom was slain. Because David temporarily lost control of himself, he temporarily lost the rule over his kingdom. It was a great price to pay for a few moments of pleasure.

But David's mourning over Absalom was not natural. Second Samuel 19 tells us that the soldiers were actually ashamed of their victory because it brought such sorrow to their king. David refused to be comforted. Why? Because he was atoning for his sins. It took the blunt speech of Joab to show the king how selfish he was. "I see," said Joab, "that you would be pleased if Absalom were alive today and all of us were dead" (2 Samuel 19:6). David's abnormal grief had so isolated him from reality that he was unable to live like a king and rule over himself and his people.

The sorrows of life do not create problems; they reveal them. Absalom's death and David's unnatural mourning revealed to the world that David had not been in control of his family and that his own sins had found him out. Instead of trying to atone for his sin, David should have trusted God for the forgiveness that he needed. That is what he did when he confessed his sin of adultery and God graciously forgave him. "You do not delight in sacrifice, or I would bring it; you do not take pleasure in burnt offerings. The sacrifices of God are a broken spirit; a broken and contrite heart, O God, you will not despise" (Psalm 51:16–17).

Today we do not bring bulls and goats; we bring excessive tears as our sacrifices. Yet God wants neither one. The comfort of God comes to those who trust the grace of God, not to those who try to earn God's comfort by unnatural sorrow. Even though our sorrows may be caused by our sins, as were David's, we can still confess those sins to the Lord, claim His forgiveness, and experience His comfort. Absalom almost stole the kingdom from David, but David almost lost it by his own foolishness. When you reign in life you have control over your own emotions; when you give way to unnatural sorrow, you get off the throne and lose control of life.

SUPERNATURAL SORROW

But the main thrust of this Beatitude is *supernatural* sorrow. Jesus is talking about repentance for sin, and that is the result of the supernatural working of God in your life. "Godly sorrow brings repentance that leads to salvation and leaves no regret, but worldly sorrow brings death" (2 Corinthians 7:10).

This godly sorrow is the logical result of the experience of the first Beatitude: "Blessed are the poor in spirit; for theirs is the kingdom of heaven." People who see their spiritual bankruptcy can respond in one of four ways. They can deny that their bankruptcy exists and, like the Pharisees, put on a front. But these people lead a life of deception, using most of their strength to pretend so that they have little energy left for living. Second, they can admit their spiritual bankruptcy and try to change things on their own. But this is a case of the poor helping the poor. Third, they can admit their need and so despair over it that they give up completely. This is "the sorrow of the world" that produces death. Judas saw he was a sinner and committed suicide. Peter saw he was a sinner and wept bitterly. That is the difference between the sorrow of the world and the godly sorrow that leads to repentance. The logical thing for people to do when they see their own spiritual need is to admit it and then *turn to God for what they need*. Those who are sincerely poor in spirit will mourn over themselves and their sins, and through this mourning they will experience the comfort of God.

We must distinguish, however, among repentance and remorse and regret. When my consciousness of sin rests only in my mind, then it is regret. When it affects my mind and my heart, it is remorse, and remorse is a dangerous thing. But when my concern over my sin brings me to the place where I am willing to turn from it and obey God—when my concern affects my *will* as well as my mind and my heart—then I have experienced true repentance.

You may remember the story about the Sunday school teacher who asked a pupil to define *repentance*, and the boy replied: "Repentance means sorrow for sin." "That's right!" said the teacher. But then a little girl spoke up: "Excuse me, but it means being sorry enough to quit!" She knew that repentance involves not only a change in feeling and thinking but also a change of the *will*. If people truly change their minds about sin, they will act differently.

The prodigal son (Luke 15) illustrates the truth perfectly; his mind, heart, and will were all involved in his repentance. His mind told him that his father's servants were better off than he was; his heart made him sick of his situation ("I perish with hunger!"), and his will motivated him to arise and go to his father. Had he sat there in the pigpen thinking how foolish he had been, it would have been regret. Had he thought about his sins and hated himself for committing them, it would have been remorse. When he said, "I will arise and go!"—and he arose and went—that was repentance. His sorrow was a godly sorrow that motivated him to return home and experience forgiveness.

About what are we supposed to repent? Obviously, we should repent of our sins. "I confess my iniquity; I am troubled by my sin" (Psalm 38:18). We must be careful that it is sin over which we sorrow and not the painful consequences of sin or the fact that we have been caught. Too many people fail to see the difference. When sinners repent of their sins and put their faith in Jesus Christ, then they are saved. This was Paul's message: "Repentance toward God, and faith toward our Lord Jesus Christ" (Acts 20:21 KJV).

Does God expect His own children to repent? I believe He does. Paul commended the believers at Corinth because they received his letter and "sorrowed to repentance" (2 Corinthians 7:9 KJV). On the other hand, Paul warned that same church that he would come and discipline those who had not repented, and certainly he was talking about professed Christians (2 Corinthians 12:21). In His last message to the church, our Lord commands His people to repent (Revelation 2:5, 16; 3:3, 19).

We must beware of an easy and comfortable dealing with our sins. It was this surface dealing with sin that cost King Saul his crown. The record is in 1 Samuel 15. First, Saul lied about his sin: "I have carried out the Lord's instructions" (v. 13). Then he made an excuse instead of a confession: It was "the people" who had disobeyed God, not Saul. Finally, Saul used religion to defend sin. He said he would use the animals that were spared as sacrifices for the Lord. Even after Samuel exposed Saul's wickedness, the king persisted in defending himself and blaming the people (vv. 20–21). And when King Saul finally said, "I have sinned" (v. 30), he still qualified his confession with a condition: "But please honor me before the elders of my people and before Israel" (v. 30). He was more concerned about his reputation than his character, what other people thought rather than what God thought.

From that point on, Saul began to lose his kingdom, and David began to gain his kingdom. It was David, not Saul, who defeated Goliath (1 Samuel 17). David slew tens of thousands of the enemy, whereas Saul slew only thousands (1 Samuel 18:7). Saul began to fear and suspect. He tried to kill David; he even turned against Jonathan, his own son. God departed from Saul, and the record closes with King Saul turning to Satan for help, inquiring of a witch (1 Samuel 28) and then dying in shame on the field of battle. Nothing leads to defeat in the Christian life like a surface dealing with sin.

This does not mean that the disobedient believer must wallow in self-reproach and condemnation, because even that attitude could be sinful. Paul told the Corinthians to forgive the man who had been guilty of sin, "so that he will not be overwhelmed by excessive sorrow" (2 Corinthians 2:7). Why? "In order that Satan might not outwit us" (2 Corinthians 2:11). Satan is the "accuser of our brothers" (Revelation 12:10); he likes nothing better than to remind the saints of their sins and make them miserable to the point of giving up.

There are two extremes to avoid when it comes to dealing with our sins: being too easy on ourselves and being too hard on ourselves. Either extreme will cost us the enjoyment of our kingdom. King Saul was too easy on his sins, and he lost the crown; David was too hard on himself at the death of Absalom, and he almost lost the crown.

As Christians we must repent of our sins. That means more than admitting them and trying to explain or excuse them. It means admitting them, looking upon them the way God does, abhorring them, and turning from them. "A broken and contrite heart, O God, you will not despise" (Psalm 51:17). Simply quoting 1 John 1:9 in a glib manner is not true repentance. That promise is not an excuse for sin; it is an encouragement to believers who want to get rid of sin. "If we confess our sins, he is faithful and just and will forgive us our sins and purify us from all unrighteousness." That word *confess* literally means "to say the same thing." If I am to be forgiven, I must agree with God's verdict about my sins. King Saul said, "I have sinned" and then proceeded to argue with the prophet and make excuses. King David said, "I have sinned," and the prophet said to him, "The Lord has taken away your sin. You are not going to die" (2 Samuel 12:13).

It is necessary for us to repent of our sins, but that is only the beginning. We all can mourn over our sins, but not too many people mourn over the fact that they are sinners. We should show sorrow not only for what we do but also for what we are. This kind of sorrow seems strange to the superficial Christian, but it was not strange to godly men and women of the Bible and the saints of church history. "Surely I was sinful at birth, sinful from the time my mother conceived me" (Psalm 51:5) was not David's excuse for his disobedience. It was his expression of a deeper repentance. "I am not only sorry for what I did, but I am also sorry for what I am." As you read Psalm 51, you realize that David was confessing the fact that his being was polluted by sin. His "inner parts" were defiled (v. 6), his ears no longer heard joy (v. 8), his heart was dirty, and his spirit needed renewal (v. 10)—even his tongue and his lips were paralyzed by sin (vv. 14–15). His eyes saw nothing but sin: "My sin is always before me" (v. 3). Here is a man who repented of his sins—but not in a superficial way: He exposed every part of his being to the searchlight of God.

But this mourning goes even deeper. We repent not only of what we do and what we are, but we also mourn over what sin does in this world. Jeremiah wept over the sins of his people. Jesus wept over the sins of Jerusalem. Paul wept as he ministered in the churches. All of creation is groaning because of sin, and the believer joins in that groaning (Romans 8:22–23). Although we thank God that He gives to us in this world "everything for our enjoyment" (1 Timothy 6:17), we also weep because our Father's world has been so polluted and plundered by sin. The present crisis in ecology is but a symptom of that deeper crisis. Many people weep over the loss of precious resources and the marring of irreplaceable beauty, but few weep over the godless rebellion in people's hearts that has caused this crisis.

We not only mourn over sin in our lives and in the world God made, but we also mourn over sin in the lives of others. When a member of the church at Corinth was living in shameless incest, the church members should have mourned; instead, they boasted of their open-mindedness (1 Corinthians 5). "And you are proud!

Shouldn't you rather have been filled with grief?" Paul scolded (v. 2). The Greek word translated *grief* means "to mourn as for the dead." If the believers at Corinth had truly mourned because of that sin, they would have lovingly dealt with the offender and brought him to a place of repentance. "Brothers, if someone is caught in a sin, you who are spiritual should restore him gently" (Galatians 6:1).

Christians who are able to deal with sin in their own lives can be trusted to deal with sin in the lives of others. They will be neither too easy nor too hard. It is often the case that those who are too easy on themselves will be hard on others. Saul excused himself for disobeying God, yet he threatened to kill his son Jonathan for disobeying his own foolish commandment (1 Samuel 14:24–25). David was excessively hard on himself and yet too easy on Absalom. Maintaining a balance in dealing with sin—our own and others'—requires the wisdom of God and the leading of His Spirit. Satan welcomes either extreme. If we are too easy in dealing with sin, the matter is not settled to the glory of God; if we are too hard, it could result in "excessive sorrow" and defeat.

It may seem strange, but this mourning over sin can go even deeper. We mourn over what we do, what we are, and what sin has wrought in this world and in the lives of others, but we also mourn over our mourning. This may sound neurotic, but it is not. As we grow in grace, we realize more and more how inadequate we are to face God and deal with our sins. Jeremiah was not satisfied with his mourning. "Oh, that my head were a spring of water and my eyes a fountain of tears! I would weep day and night for the slain of my people" (Jeremiah 9:1). "This is why I weep and my eyes overflow with tears" (Lamentations 1:16). As we read Lamentations, we realize how deeply Jeremiah's heart was moved because of sin, and the sin was not even his own.

When you and I learn how to mourn, then we will have a deeper understanding of the sinfulness of sin and the graciousness of God.

SPIRITUAL COMFORT

Christ promises comfort to those who mourn, but what kind of comfort is it? You can be sure that it is far deeper than sympathy, expressed by drying another's tears or enfolding a child in arms of love. Our English word *comfort* comes from two Latin words that mean "with strength" (The words *fortify* and *fortress* carry the same meaning.) We are prone to confuse *comfort* and *sympathy*, but they are not identical. To sympathize means "to feel with," whereas to comfort means "to encourage, to give strength." Our mourning puts us in touch with the eternal resources of God, and the result is God's comfort. "When I called, you answered me; you made me bold and stouthearted" (Psalm 138:3).

Our God is the "God of all comfort" (2 Corinthians 1:3). His attitude toward us is not one of hostility but one of love and encouragement. He is not against us; He is *for* us. This is one of the emphases in Romans 8. The Holy Spirit makes intercession for us (v. 26). God the Father delivered up His Son for us (v. 32). God the Son is making intercession for us (v. 34). No wonder Paul cried, "If God is for us, who can be against us?" (v. 31). "'For I know the plans that I have for you,' declares the Lord, 'plans for welfare and not for calamity to give you a future and a hope'" (Jeremiah 29:11 NASB). Our comfort and encouragement is God Himself. "But David encouraged himself in the Lord his God" (1 Samuel 30:6 KJV). How different from King Saul, who refused to mourn over his sin. "Immediately Saul fell full length on the ground, filled with fear" (1 Samuel 28:20).

We have also the comfort of the Scriptures. "For everything that was written in the past was written to teach us, so that through endurance and the encouragement of the Scriptures we might have hope. May the God who gives endurance and encouragement give you a spirit of unity among yourselves as you follow Christ Jesus" (Romans 15:4–5). The same Word that reveals our sins also reveals the grace and forgiveness of God. Nathan said to David, "You are the man!" (2 Samuel 12:7). But he also said, "The Lord has taken away your sin" (v. 13). The sinful woman mourned at Jesus' feet, and He said to her, "Your sins are forgiven . . . Your faith has saved you; go in peace" (Luke 7:48, 50). To the woman taken in the act of adultery He said, "Neither do I condemn you . . . Go now and leave your life of sin" (John 8:11).

God also gives us the comfort of the Holy Spirit, for the Spirit is the Comforter (John 14:16). He is the great encourager, the one who puts strength in our souls. In the Scriptures we have the *objective* source of comfort, and in the Spirit within, we have the *subjective* source of comfort. The same Spirit who wrote the Word lives in our hearts, and He opens up the Scriptures so that His comfort comes into our lives. Only those who have experienced the comforting ministry of the Holy Spirit can understand this holy experience.

Finally, God comforts us through His people. Often the Holy Spirit uses another Christian to bring us the encouragement that we need. God comforted Paul by the coming of Titus (2 Corinthians 7:6), and Titus comforted Paul by reporting that the problems in the church were being solved. In fact, one reason we as Christians go through difficulties is so that we might be able to experience the comfort of God and then share that comfort with others. God "comforts us in all our troubles, so that we can comfort those in any trouble with the comfort we ourselves have received from God" (2 Corinthians 1:4). This does not mean that we must experience exactly the same trials to be of encouragement to others, because God's comfort enables us to encourage those who are in "any trouble." God's comfort is not a luxury for us to hoard; it is a necessity that we must share. "Carry each other's burdens, and in this way you will fulfill the law of Christ" (Galatians 6:2).

THE MAN OF SORROWS

Our Lord was a "man of sorrows, and familiar with suffering" (Isaiah 53:3). He knew what it was to mourn, not over His own sins, of course, because He had no sin (2 Corinthians 5:21), but over the sins of the world and the havoc sin wrought in the world. He wept at the tomb of Lazarus, even though He knew He would raise Lazarus from the dead. In the garden Jesus wept "with loud cries and tears" (Hebrews 5:7) as He faced the cross, knowing that the eternal sorrow for sin would come upon Him there. What a paradox that He should suffer such great sorrow, at the same time looking to "the joy set before him" (Hebrews 12:2).

That Jesus Christ was the Man of Sorrows suggests that, as we experience true mourning for sin, we become more like Christ. It is significant that people believed that Jesus was Jeremiah returned from the grave (Matthew 16:14), because Jeremiah, too, was a man of sorrows and acquainted with grief. "Is it nothing to you, all you who pass by? Look around and see. Is any suffering like my suffering?" (Lamentations 1:12). Of course we must not major in mourning; there is also the "joy of the Lord," which is our strength (Nehemiah 8:10). But as we pray, we see ourselves (as did Abraham) "but dust and ashes" (Genesis 18:27). As we see God's blessing, we confess with Peter: "Go away from me, Lord; I am a sinful man!" (Luke 5:8). There is always new mourning and there is always new comfort, and this process makes us more like the Master.

The tears of believers work *for* them and are an investment in future joys. Not all of our comfort will be given today. "Weeping may remain for a night, but rejoicing comes in the morning" (Psalm 30:5). "Those who sow in tears will reap with songs of joy" (Psalm 126:5). "He will wipe every tear from their eyes" (Revelation 21:4). Psalm 56:8 teaches us that none of our tears will go unnoticed by God: "List my tears on your scroll—are they not in your record?" If God sees the sparrow fall, will He not also see our tears fall? Heaven will be a place of no tears, but hell will be a place of nothing but tears. It was Jesus who said, "There will be weeping and gnashing of teeth" (Matthew 8:12).

There is one way that the believer will never become like the Man of Sorrows: He never wept for Himself; He always wept for others. He said to the sympathetic women of Jerusalem, "Do not weep for me; weep for yourselves and for your children" (Luke 23:28). Until we see Him in glory and become like Him, we will have to weep for ourselves. "Not that I have already obtained all this, or have already been made perfect" (Philippians 3:12). But as we weep, we can be sure of His promise: "Blessed are those who mourn, for they will be comforted."

Blessed are the meek, for they will inherit the earth.
(Matthew 5:5)

*Take my yoke upon you and learn from me, for I am gentle
and humble in heart, and you will find rest for your souls.*
(Matthew 11:29)

*Now the man Moses was very meek, above all
the men which were upon the face of the earth.*
(Numbers 12:3 KJV)

The fruit of the Spirit is . . . meekness.
(Galatians 5:22–23 KJV)

*With all lowliness and meekness, with longsuffering,
forbearing one another in love.*
(Ephesians 4:2 KJV)

Receive with meekness the engrafted word.
(James 1:21 KJV)

5

THE MEEK

MEEKNESS IS NOT WEAKNESS

Many people misunderstand the meaning of meekness because they have the idea that meekness is weakness. We live in a world that worships power and rejects any evidence of weakness; perhaps this explains why many successful people will have little or nothing to do with the Christian faith. They have heard about "Gentle Jesus, meek and mild," and they want nothing to do with Him. The ladder of success in today's world is climbed with heavy steps; there is no place for timidity.

But meekness is not weakness or timidity. Meekness is power under control. Certainly nobody could accuse Moses of being a weak, timid man, yet God identified him as the meekest man on the face of the earth. Jesus was the most courageous man ever to walk among humans, and yet He said, "I am meek and lowly in heart" (Matthew 11:29 KJV). Both Moses and Jesus faced difficult, dangerous situations and came through victoriously because they exercised power under control.

God has given us the ability to become angry. Nowhere does the Bible honor the spineless person who is unable (or unwilling) to exercise the right kind of anger. "In your anger do not sin" (Ephesians 4:26). There is a sinless anger, such as when Moses came down from Mount Sinai and saw his people reveling in sin or when Jesus strode into the temple and majestically cleansed His Father's house. There is a godless anger that destroys, but there is a godly anger that builds up. Two verses from Proverbs explain the difference: "Better a patient man than a warrior, a man who controls his temper than one who takes a city (Proverbs 16:32). That is power under control. "Like a city whose walls are broken down is a man who lacks self-control" (Proverbs 25:28). That is power out of control.

Someone has said, "Temper is such a wonderful thing that it's a shame to lose it!" We temper steel to make it stronger. People who lose their temper lose control of themselves and stop living like kings. A successful businessman, Roger Babson, once said, "The best administrator is the governor of his temper."

"Anyone can become angry," wrote Aristotle in his *Nicomachean Ethics*. "That is easy. But to be angry with the right person, to the right degree, at the right time, for the right purpose, and in the right way—this is not easy." What the great philosopher was talking about was meekness—power under control. Anger is power, just as fire is power. (We sometimes say, "His anger flared up!") When fire is under control, it is our servant and accomplishes great things for us. But when fire is out of control, it becomes our master, and the result is destruction. So it is with anger.

"There is nothing wrong with losing my temper," a lady once told evangelist Billy Sunday. "I blow up, and then it's over with."

"So does a shotgun," the evangelist replied, "but look at the damage that's left behind."

The Greek word that is translated *meekness* was a familiar word to the people in Jesus' day. It was used to describe a soothing medicine. Doctors gave patients who wrestled with a fever medication to quiet them down and relieve their high temperature so that they could sleep. Sailors also used the word to describe a gentle breeze. Have you ever been exhausted on a hot day and then felt a cooling breeze blow on your body? It is refreshing. But doctors and sailors were not the only ones to use that word, because farmers used it too. It was used to describe a colt that has been broken. Every colt has to be broken, or it cannot fulfill its function on the farm. Somebody has to break the colt so that its power can be channeled into constructive work.

Look at these three illustrations: medicine, wind, and a colt. What do they all have in common? Power! Medicine has power to work in the body to calm nerves, kill germs, strengthen organs, and promote healing. The wind also has power. Hurricanes embody the power of wind, and the infamous Katrina devastated the U.S. Gulf Coast in 2005, displacing over 700,000 people whose homes were destroyed. That is power. If you have ever watched a cowboy on a bucking bronco, you know that a horse is a powerful animal. But the medicine, wind, and horse must keep their power under control, otherwise they will do damage. The proper dosage of medicine can promote healing, but an overdose may kill. A summer breeze is a delightful thing, but a hurricane only destroys. A broken horse can give both work and pleasure to its master, but a horse out of control is dangerous. All of these have power, and when that power is under control, it is called meekness.

MEET THE MEEK

Perhaps the best way to understand meekness is to see it at work in the lives of people like us.

When Abraham left Ur of the Chaldees, he took his nephew Lot with him, and it was not long before there was a family disagreement. "And quarreling arose between Abram's herdsmen and the herdsmen of Lot" (Genesis 13:7). If you were Abraham, what would you have done? Certainly Abraham had the authority to tell Lot to pack up and get moving. After all, Abraham was God's chosen servant; he was even called the friend of God. It was Abraham whom God called and with whom God had made His covenant; Lot was simply a tagalong. Abraham had power over Lot, but he kept that power under control. He exercised meekness.

> So Abram said to Lot, "Let's not have any quarreling between you and me, or between your herdsmen and mine, for we are brothers. Is not the whole land before you? Let's part company. If you go to the left, I'll go to the right; if you go to the right, I'll go to the left" (GENESIS 13:8–9).

Had Abraham been like most of us, he would have said, "I am the elder of this clan, and I get first choice!" To many people, that kind of an attitude would have been exercising leadership. To God, it would have been committing sin. Abraham had power, but his power was under control, and he gave Lot first choice. "Honor one another above yourselves" (Romans 12:10). "Let each esteem others more important than themselves" (Philippians 2:3, literal translation). Because Abraham was surrendered to God, he was not afraid to submit to Lot. Abraham knew that his own inheritance was secure in the Lord and that no decision on the part of his nephew could ever rob him of anything that God had for him. Abraham had power, but his power was under control, so God kept His promise and enabled Abraham to "inherit the earth."

Joseph is another vivid illustration of meekness. Mistreated by his brothers, Joseph was sold into Egypt as a slave. Then he was put into prison when his master's wife falsely accused him of making sexual advances towards her. But one day Joseph was elevated to become the prime minister of Egypt. He had the power to take revenge against his master's wife, but there is no record that he ever did. And then his brothers showed up, begging for food, and although Joseph could have refused them or punished them, he did not. To be sure, he dealt with them so that they eventually confessed their sins and gave evidence of true repentance; but in the end Joseph refused to hurt them. He had power over them, but he kept his power under control.

Remember: Meekness does not show itself when we are wrong but when we are right. Meekness is not the shamefaced boy who is caught with his hand in the cookie jar. Meekness is not embarrassment when I am caught doing something wrong. Meekness is power under control. It reveals itself when I am right and when I have the power to hurt someone who is wrong.

I think of David as another illustration of meekness. David's greatest victories were not with his hands but with his heart. In 1 Samuel 24, Saul blundered into the cave where David and his men were hiding. With one flashing stroke of his sword, David could have killed Saul and taken the throne. In fact, some of David's men urged him to do just that, putting an end to the man who was chasing them and seeking their lives. Instead of cutting off Saul's head, David quietly cut off the skirt of Saul's robe; even that action made him feel guilty. David had the power to kill Saul, but he kept his power under control.

There was another episode in David's life that reveals his meekness in an even greater measure. It is recorded in 2 Samuel 16. David's son Absalom took over the kingdom and forced his father to flee into the wilderness. During that difficult time, one of Saul's men, Shimei, cursed David and threw stones at him. Abishai, David's nephew, said to the king, "Let me go over and cut off his head" (v. 9). That would have been a reasonable thing to do in that day, but David would not permit it. His only answer was, "Leave him alone; let him curse, for the Lord has told him to" (v. 11). That is power under control.

It is likely that Saul would have killed David had he caught him in the cave, and no doubt Saul would have killed Shimei as well. The difference between those two kings is not that one had power and the other did not, for both had power. The difference is that David's power was under control. He was a meek man. David used his authority to build up people; Saul used people to build up his authority. At one time, Saul was going to kill his own son for a trivial matter, just to show the people how powerful he was (1 Samuel 14:36–45). David was willing to die for his own son, even though Absalom was a rebel (2 Samuel 18:33).

Of course, the greatest example of meekness is the Lord Jesus Christ. "He was led like a lamb to the slaughter, and as a sheep before her shearers is silent, so he did not open his mouth" (Isaiah 53:7). "When they hurled their insults at him, he did not retaliate; when he suffered, he made no threats. Instead, he entrusted himself to him who judges justly" (1 Peter 2:23). It took more power for Jesus to submit than for Peter to draw out his sword and fight. Peter's action was natural; what our Lord did was supernatural. Jesus exercised power under control. He could have summoned legions of angels, but instead he "became obedient to death—even death on a cross!" (Philippians 2:8).

ARE YOU MEEK?

How can you and I tell whether we are meek?

Perhaps the simplest answer is a question: Are we exercising self-control? Is our power under control? We have physical power, mental power, emotional power, and even spiritual power. Are we keeping all of this power under control?

But I believe that the best test of meekness is found in the word *attitude*. For example, what is our attitude toward the circumstances of life? When Jesus said, "Blessed are the meek, for they will inherit the earth," He was quoting from Psalm 37:11: "But the meek will inherit the land and enjoy great peace." When you read Psalm 37, you discover that the writer was going through a great deal of trouble. Evil unbelievers were trying to cut him down. They were slandering him and trying to ruin his reputation. In fact, they were plotting against him and trying to take his life. Perhaps you and I have never had our lives threatened, but we have experienced difficult circumstances. How do we respond to them? What is our attitude toward the difficulties of life?

Too many people respond—or react—to the difficulties of life by fretting. "Do not fret," says the opening verse of Psalm 37, and it is repeated in verse 8: "Refrain from anger and turn from wrath; do not fret—it leads only to evil." The normal thing to do when people attack you is to get angry, fret over it, and fight back, but this is not the spiritual thing to do. Meek people submit themselves and their enemies to God and let Him handle the problem. Look at the admonitions in Psalm 37: "Trust in the Lord; . . . Delight yourself in the Lord; . . . Be still before the Lord and wait patiently for him; . . . Refrain from anger; . . . Turn from evil and do good" (vv. 3–4, 7–8, 27). The meek center their attention and affection on the Lord, not on themselves or their adversary. When you find yourself fretting because of people or circumstances, you can be sure that you have lost your meekness.

Another test of meekness is one's attitude toward God's Word. James 1:19 commands us to be "quick to listen, slow to speak and slow to become angry." James 1:21 (KJV) commands us to "receive with meekness the engrafted [imparted] word." James wrote his letter to a group of Christians who were at war with each other. "What causes fights and quarrels among you?"(4:1). One reason for their division was a stubborn attitude toward God's Word. Instead of receiving God's Word with meekness—like planting seed in soft soil—they were arguing and becoming angry. They were not "slow to speak and slow to become angry." The meek Christian submits to the Word of God and receives it gladly into a prepared heart.

Again we see the contrast between Saul and David. When Samuel gave Saul God's message, the king argued with it and tried to excuse himself. He blamed the people, and he even blamed Samuel. "I saw that the men were scattering, and that you did not come at the set time, and that the Philistines were assembling at Michmash" (1 Samuel 13:11). Later, God gave Saul another chance to live like a king, and again he failed. Instead of slaying the enemy as he was commanded (1 Samuel 15), he kept the best for himself and then blamed the people. "The soldiers took sheep and cattle from the plunder, . . . in order to sacrifice them to the Lord your God at Gilgal" (v. 21). Saul was not a meek man; he refused to submit to the Word of God.

But David submitted and "received with meekness the engrafted word. "David's chaplain, Nathan, took his life in his hands when he confronted the king with his adultery and murder (2 Samuel 12), for David was a backslidden man and could have ordered the prophet to be killed. Nathan told the touching story about the one little ewe lamb that the rich man stole from the poor man. Bravely, Nathan said, "You are the man" —and waited. Would David's anger be kindled against his prophet? No, because David was a meek man, and he received God's Word without arguing, making excuses, or defending himself. "I have sinned against the Lord" (v. 13). He was a man after God's own heart.

The third test of meekness is one's attitude toward fellow Christians who sin. Do I receive the news gleefully and start to spread it? Am I pleased that they have sinned because their fall makes my walk look better? "Brothers, if someone is caught in a sin, you who are spiritual should restore him gently. But watch yourself, or you also may be tempted" (Galatians 6:1). When a Christian has fallen into sin, I have the power to hurt him or her, but meekness is power under control. I also have the power to help. "Restore such an one." Doctors used that word *restore* in Paul's day; it means "to set a broken bone." When a Christian falls into sin, it affects the body of Christ the way a broken bone affects your physical body; it must be restored. My first response to a fellow believer's sin ought to be sorrow and pity and then a desire to help him or her get back into fellowship with God. Shimei threw stones at David when David was at his weakest physically and politically, yet David proved himself to be the stronger man spiritually. Later, when David's throne was restored, Shimei came to beg forgiveness, and David forgave him. He restored him in a spirit of meekness (2 Samuel 19:16–23).

A broken bone is painful, and setting it can be even more painful than the break itself. Doctors do not use a crowbar and a pipe wrench to set a broken bone; they use power under control. That is meekness.

A fourth test of meekness is one's attitude toward division in the church. "As a prisoner for the Lord, then, I urge you to live a life worthy of the calling you have received. Be completely humble and gentle; be patient, bearing with one another in love. Make every effort to keep the unity of the Spirit through the bond of peace (Ephesians 4:1–3). There are people in every church who always want to take sides and divide God's people.

When I was a boy in the junior department of Sunday school, I remember hearing a teacher say, "Well, there's a business meeting this week, and I'm going to be there loaded for bear!" The next Sunday a number of people were missing from the services, and I discovered that the "hunter" had shot off his mouth and there had been a church split.

Christians who exercise meekness are not interested in taking sides; they are interested in "being diligent to preserve the unity of the Spirit in the bond of peace" (Ephesians 4:3 NASB). They follow the example of Abraham: "Let's not have any quarreling between you and me . . . for we are brothers" (Genesis 13:8).

The fifth test of meekness in our lives concerns our attitude toward those people who disagree with us. "The servant of the Lord must not strive; but be gentle unto all men, apt to teach, patient, in meekness instructing those that oppose themselves; if God peradventure will give them repentance to the acknowledging of the truth" (2 Timothy 2:24–25 NASB). It is possible to win arguments and lose friends—and souls!

The poet Oliver Goldsmith said of Samuel Johnson, England's "czar of literature": "There is no arguing with Johnson, for if his pistol misses fire, he knocks you down with the butt end of it!" Some Christians are like that. "Watch out for So-and-So," a friend warned me. "He uses a cannon to kill a mosquito!" It is a mark of meekness—and maturity—when we realize that good people disagree. Even the person who opposes the Word of God has a better chance of being convinced if we have a meek and gentle spirit. I like J. W. C. Wand's translation of 2 Timothy 2:27: "The Lord's servant must not quarrel, but be gentle to all, good at teaching, slow to take offense, one who can reduce his opponents by the mildness of his manners."

Finally, what is my attitude toward the unsaved? "But in your hearts set apart Christ as Lord. Always be prepared to give an answer to everyone who asks you to give the reason for the hope that you have. But do this with gentleness [meekness] and respect" (1 Peter 3:15). Peter is warning against arguing with lost souls and using the Bible as a club to beat them down. He is telling us to be witnesses and not prosecuting attorneys. Too often we use high-pressure salesmanship methods in our zeal to win souls, but that is power out of control. Jesus could have overpowered Nicodemus or crushed the woman of Samaria, but instead He patiently led them into the truth of the Word of God.

MEEKNESS GROWS IN TRIALS

How can the believer go about cultivating this grace of meekness? Galatians 5:23 tells us that meekness is not something that we manufacture; it is part of the fruit of the Spirit. Fruit is not manufactured; fruit must be cultivated. There was a time when Moses, the meekest man on earth, became angry with an enemy and killed him. God had to put Moses on the backside of the desert for forty years, taking care of his father-in-law's sheep, in order to prepare him for his ministry. Alone in the desert, caring for the meekest of animals, Moses began to learn meekness. He was the adopted son of Pharaoh's daughter, educated in all the wisdom of Egypt, and yet he became a shepherd.

We cultivate meekness in the difficult experiences of life. Think of what Moses had to endure as he led the people of Israel. No sooner was the nation delivered from Egypt than the people began to complain, and they complained for the next forty years until that generation died. They complained about the way God led them and about the way He fed them. They rebelled against

Moses' authority. They tried to organize a party to return to Egypt. When Moses finally brought them to the border of the Promised Land, they refused to go in. All of his sacrifice and work was for nothing. No, it was not for nothing, for Moses was growing in grace and cultivating the wonderful grace of meekness. Moses had always had power, but it was not under control. It was in the school of hard knocks that he learned to be meek.

King Saul never learned meekness because he always tried to scheme his way out of the difficulties of life. Instead of trials bringing out the best in him, they brought out his worst. And he always had an excuse ready whenever Samuel showed up. "An excuse," said Billy Sunday, "is the skin of a reason, stuffed with a lie." People who are good at excuses are rarely good at anything else. But David profited from the trials of life and, in spite of his failures (and we all have them), learned how to be meek. Saul tried to use his own authority to make himself great, but David said to God, "You stoop down to make me great" (Psalm 18:35). As David reviewed the trials of his life, he looked back and saw how gentle God had been. Anybody can submit to harshness, but it takes a great person to submit to gentleness. It takes a person whose heart is gentle and whose attitude is characterized by meekness.

The Saul of the Old Testament never learned meekness, but the Saul of the New Testament did. When Paul the apostle was Saul of Tarsus, he possessed great power. And he used that power to persecute and even to kill. "It is hard for you to kick against the goads," Jesus said to him (Acts 26:14 NASB), suggesting that Saul was like a wild animal that had never been broken. But God broke him, and a spirit of meekness came into his life.

As a Christian and an apostle, Paul had more power and authority than ever before, but he used that power for the good of others and the glory of God. He had learned meekness. The situation in the Corinthian church, for example, was enough to test the patience of Job, yet when you read Paul's Corinthian letters you see power under control. "What do you prefer?" he asks in 1 Corinthians 4:21. "Shall I come to you with a whip, or in love and with a gentle spirit?" In his second letter he beseeches them "by the meekness and gentleness of Christ" (10:1). To the believers in Galatia, Ephesus, and Colosse, Paul urged the cultivation of meekness, and when he wrote to the pastors—Timothy and Titus—he reminded them to show meekness. Like Elijah on Mount Horeb, Paul had learned that God was not in the wind or the earthquake or the fire, but in "the still, small voice." That is power under control.

You and I must make the choice: Will we submit in the difficulties of life and cultivate meekness, or will we rebel and produce hardness? The fruit of the Spirit is meekness, but it takes time for the fruit to grow, and the fruit grows best in the storms of life.

THE MEEK ARE ENRICHED

From the world's point of view, meekness is the first step toward failure. Unless you toot your own horn, wave your own flag, and promote your own goals, you will never get anywhere in today's competitive world. Centuries ago, the Athenian statesman Pericles described the situation perfectly when he said, "Fishes in the sea, . . . as men do a-land; the great ones eat up the little ones."

But from the divine point of view, self-promotion is the fastest way to failure. "Although you were once small in your own eyes," Samuel said to King Saul, "did you not become the head of the tribes of Israel? The Lord anointed you king over Israel" (1 Samuel 15:17). When Saul was little, God made him great, but when Saul made himself great, God made him nothing. Saul lost his crown.

But David showed a spirit of meekness, so God gave him the crown. "The Spirit of the Lord came upon David . . . [but] the Spirit of the Lord had departed from Saul" (1 Samuel 16:13–14). Because David submitted to God, he grew in the trials of life and was prepared by God to sit on the throne and rule Israel. Both David and Jesus, the Son of David, had to suffer and be rejected before they reigned; the same pattern is duplicated in our lives. We reign in life by resigning our lives. "For whoever wants to save his life will lose it, but whoever loses his life for me will find it" (Matthew 16:25).

"Blessed are the meek, for they will inherit the earth." What does that mean? Does it mean that meek people escape the difficulties of life? I don't believe so, because Moses was meek and yet he faced one difficulty after another. To answer the question we must go back to Psalm 37, where the original statement is found.

The conflict in this psalm is between the righteous and the wicked. (Note the repetition of "the wicked" in verses 10, 12, 14, 20–21, 28, 32, 34–35, 38, and 40.) It appears that the wicked are winning and the righteous are losing. James Russell Lowell phrased it, "Truth forever on the scaffold, wrong forever on the throne."

What can the righteous do in such a dangerous and difficult situation? Fret? No. God said, "Do not fret because of evil men" (Psalm 37:1). Fight? No. The Lord stands by to protect the righteous and fight their battle for them. "The salvation of the righteous comes from the Lord; he is their stronghold in time of trouble" (v. 39).

Then what should the righteous do? Meekly submit to God's will by trusting in the Lord (v. 3), delighting in the Lord (v. 4), committing their way unto the Lord (v. 5), and resting in the Lord (v. 7). The result is that they will "inherit the earth," which simply means that they do not have to be afraid of anybody or anything because God is in control of them and their circumstances. To

inherit the earth means to reign as king over yourself and your circumstances through the power of the Holy Spirit. "A little while,
and the wicked will be no more; though you look for them, they
will not be found. But the meek will inherit the land and enjoy
great peace" (vv. 10–11).

When you are meek, you seek nothing for yourself, and when
you seek nothing for yourself, God gives you all things. Saul's self-
seeking cost him his crown, but David's submission gave him the
kingdom. Something else is true: Meekness means power under
control, and when you can control yourself, everything belongs to
you. If you can reign in peace over the kingdom within you, then
God will give you all you need in the kingdom without.

The saddest event in David's life, his sin with Bathsheba, helps
to illustrate this principle. Second Samuel 11:1 says, "At the time
when kings go off to war . . . David remained in Jerusalem." He was
not living like a king. Not only had he taken off his armor but he
had also taken off his crown. The sad result is recorded in the rest of
the chapter: adultery, deceit, murder, sin covered and not confessed.
About a year later, Nathan rebuked David for his sins and reminded
the king of how much God had given him. "I gave your master's
house to you, and your master's wives into your arms. I gave you
the house of Israel and Judah. And if all this had been too little, I
would have given you even more"(2 Samuel 12:8). God was saying
through Nathan, "David, when you were meek, I gave you blessing
after blessing. But when you became proud and disobeyed My word,
you started to lose. It is the meek who inherit, not the proud. If you
had remained meek before Me, I would have given you all that you
needed and desired and more. But now I cannot do it."

The meek own everything because they are submitted to the
God who made everything and controls everything; God is their
Father. "All things are yours, whether Paul or Apollos or Cephas

or the world or life or death or the present or the future—all are yours, and you are of Christ, and Christ is of God" (1 Corinthians 3:21–23). "Having nothing, and yet possessing everything" (2 Corinthians 6:10).

Again, our Lord Jesus Christ is the perfect illustration of this truth. Because He was "meek and lowly in heart," He never worried about the people or the circumstances in the world. You never find Him fretting. Often you find the disciples fretting and even fearing, but never Jesus. He never fretted about the storms because He knew His Father was in control. In fact, He slept in the storm! He never fretted about food. The disciples asked, "Where can we find enough bread to feed this hungry crowd?" (John 6:5, paraphrase). But Jesus was not worried because He knew His Father could provide all the bread they needed and more. When the soldiers came to arrest Him, Jesus willingly submitted because He knew His Father was in control. "Shall I not drink the cup the Father has given me?" (John 18:11).

Those who cannot control themselves are never satisfied. There is a restlessness in their hearts that robs them of the joys that are found in the blessings of God. "Thou hast made us for Thyself," said Augustine, "and our hearts are restless until they rest in Thee." "Be still before the Lord," commands Psalm 37:7, and verse 11 promises, "The meek will inherit the land." Meekness is the secret of possessing everything. And when you possess everything, you do not have to fret over what others have or what they are doing. King Saul's restlessness was caused by his envy of David, and he literally killed himself chasing David and trying to keep him from getting the crown. Saul's power was not under control, and it destroyed him.

"The meek will inherit the land." You inherit something because somebody dies and leaves a bequest to you in their will.

In this case, it is we who die—die to self—that we might grow in meekness; as we grow in meekness, we share the rich inheritance that we have in Christ. There is no need for us to assert ourselves to impress others, boast about ourselves, or even defend ourselves, because the Father has all that under His control. The meek person is never envious of others because of what they have. "Better the little that the righteous have than the wealth of many wicked" (Psalm 37:16). "I was young and now I am old, yet I have never seen the righteous forsaken or their children begging bread" (Psalm 37:25).

The great enemy of meekness is impatience. This is why the psalmist admonishes us: "Wait for the Lord and keep his way. He will exalt you to inherit the land" (v. 34). Joseph waited on the Lord, and one day he was exalted and inherited the land. David waited on the Lord and endured the persecution of Saul, and one day God exalted him to inherit the land. The meek do not fret or fight; they simply submit and wait, knowing that God's timing is perfect. "The testing of your faith develops perseverance. Perseverance must finish its work so that you may be mature and complete, not lacking anything" (James 1:3–4). Not lacking anything? That means having everything!

"Blessed are the meek, for they will inherit the earth."

Blessed are those who hunger and thirst for righteousness,
for they will be filled.
(MATTHEW 5:6)

•

As the deer pants for streams of water, so my soul pants
for you, O God. My soul thirsts for God, for the living God.
When can I go and meet with God?
(PSALM 42:1–2)

•

O God, you are my God, earnestly I seek you;
my soul thirsts for you, my body longs for you,
in a dry and weary land where there is no water.
(PSALM 63:1)

•

Come, all you who are thirsty, come to the waters;
and you who have no money, come, buy and eat! Come,
buy wine and milk without money and without cost.
Why spend money on what is not bread, and your labor on
what does not satisfy? Listen, listen to me, and eat what is
good, and your soul will delight in the richest of fare.
(ISAIAH 55:1–2)

6

THE HUNGRY AND THIRSTY

Food and water are necessities, not luxuries. This was especially true in Palestine in Jesus' day. Both food and water were used carefully and never wasted. The owning of a well and the cultivation of a field were matters of life and death. So when Jesus linked together hunger, thirst, and righteousness, He was telling the people that righteousness is not a luxury; it is a necessity. Our physical life depends upon food and water; our spiritual life depends upon righteousness.

HUNGER

It has been said that human beings are what they eat. This principle is true not only of the body but also of the soul. The outer person depends upon food and water, and the inner person depends upon righteousness. The inner person of the spirit has appetites that must be satisfied, and if those appetites are not satisfied with the spiritual food that God has provided, then that inner person becomes sickly and weak. If the inner person is to function as it should, it must be fed.

The inner person has a sense of sight. Paul prayed for the Ephesians that the "eyes of [their] heart may be enlightened" (Ephesians 1:18). Our Lord lamented that although His disciples had eyes they saw not (Mark 8:18). His counsel to the church at Laodicea was that they anoint their eyes with eye salve that they might see (Revelation 3:18).

The inner person also has a spiritual sense of hearing. "He who has ears, let him hear" (Matthew 13:9). Christ's sheep hear His voice and follow Him (John 10:3–4), but they will not follow the voice of a stranger (John 10:5). Immature Christians are "slow to learn" because they do not exercise their spiritual senses (Hebrews 5:11–14).

There is also a spiritual sense of taste. "Taste and see that the Lord is good!" (Psalm 34:8). "You have tasted that the Lord is good" (1 Peter 2:3). The soul has its hunger and thirst; those desires were built into humans at creation. "He has also set eternity in the hearts of men" (Ecclesiastes 3:11). Augustine said it perfectly: "Thou hast made us for Thyself, and our hearts are restless until they rest in Thee." Just as it is normal for the deer to thirst after water, so it is natural for people to thirst after God. They may not know that their thirst is for God, and they will probably try to satisfy that thirst with a substitute that will leave them with more thirst. But a thirst for God is what it is, just the same. God has put eternity in our hearts, and the temporal cannot satisfy.

Those who have trusted Christ have found the answer to that hidden hunger and thirst in their life, for Jesus Christ is the bread of life, and He alone can satisfy. "I am the bread of life. He who comes to me will never go hungry, and he who believes on me will never be thirsty" (John 6:35). Jesus told the Samaritan woman at the well, "Everyone who drinks this water will be thirsty again, but whoever drinks the water I shall give him will never thirst" (John 4:13–14).

It is good that a living being experience hunger and thirst. To begin with, hunger and thirst are evidences of life. Dead people have no appetites. Unsaved people have an appetite for sin; they are compared to dogs licking their own vomit and pigs wallowing in the mire (2 Peter 2:22). The Christian is a sheep—a clean animal—that enjoys the green pastures and the still waters. The kind of appetite we have is an indication of the kind of heart we have. The heart of the unbeliever, although it was created with a hunger for God, tries to satisfy itself with that which is not bread. Jeremiah says it most vividly: "They have forsaken me, the spring of living water, and have dug their own cisterns, broken cisterns that cannot hold water" (2:13).

The believer who hungers and thirsts after righteousness is giving evidence not only of life but also of health. One of the first symptoms of sickness is loss of appetite, and one of the first signs of regained health after sickness is the return of appetite. When the infection of unconfessed sin is at work in the lives of disobedient Christians, they lose their appetite for spiritual things. They spend their money on that which is not bread, and they feed on substitutes. But when Christians confess their sins and are restored to the fellowship, their appetite for the things of God returns.

Were it not for hunger and thirst, we would be unable to live and work. Hunger is a sign that the body needs fuel. If we could continue to live and work without knowing that we needed food and water, we would kill ourselves. Just as pain is a sign that there is something wrong with the body, so hunger and thirst are signs that the body needs something. The spiritual meaning is not difficult to see: A hunger and thirst for the things of God is preparation for life and service.

It is tragic when people hunger and thirst for the wrong things. The prodigal son yearned for excitement and popularity, and he found them in the far country. But they did not last, and he soon found himself hungry again, but this time there was nothing to satisfy the hunger. "How many of my father's hired men have food to spare, and here I am starving to death!" (Luke 15:17). He was so hungry that even bread would have satisfied him. Up till the time the famine hit him, he would have settled for nothing less than the finest luxuries the far country had to offer. First John 2:15–17 warns that our spiritual appetite can never be satisfied by the world—the desires of the flesh, the desires of the eyes, and the pride of life. All of those things are passing away, "but the man who does the will of God lives forever." This reminds us of our Lord's statement to His disciples when they returned to Sychar after going for food: "My food . . . is to do the will of him who sent me and to finish his work" (John 4:34). Jesus fed on the will of God; that is what satisfied Him.

What are the hungers in your life? What are the longings that you yearn to have satisfied? If our desires are apart from the will of God, to satisfy them means disappointment and judgment. If they are in the will of God, to satisfy them means enjoyment, growth, and fulfillment.

HOLINESS

Jesus tells us that the way to be satisfied ("filled") is to hunger and thirst after *righteousness*. It is a hunger for holiness that fills the soul and satisfies the appetite of the inner person. It is too bad that we desire lesser things, including lesser blessings. When the people of Israel were "in the desert they gave in to their craving . . . So [God] gave them what they asked for, but sent a wasting disease upon them" (Psalm 106:14–15). Had Israel listened to God's Word and cultivated an appetite for His will, God would have "fed them also with the finest of the wheat: and with honey out of the rock" (Psalm 81:16 KJV).

Theologians tell us that there are three kinds of holiness: imputed, which is justification; imparted, which is sanctification; and eternal, which is glorification. When sinners trust Christ, they are declared righteous; this is imputed holiness. As a result of this decision, their lives change, and they share imparted holiness. The righteousness of Christ becomes a part of their daily lives. The person who professes salvation but practices sin is not born of God (1 John 4:1–10). The Christian is not only justified by faith (Romans 5:10) but is justified unto life (Romans 5:18). Justification is much more than a legal matter recorded on the books of heaven. It is a personal matter that involves a living relationship with God and results in a living revelation of God in our everyday lives.

But what is holiness? To the Pharisees, holiness was conformity to rules; it was an external thing that completely overlooked the needs of the inner person. That explains why Jesus warned, "Unless your righteousness surpasses that of the Pharisees and the teachers of the law, you will certainly not enter the kingdom of heaven" (Matthew 5:20). A mere external piety born of pride and nurtured by the praise of others is not holiness. If the Beatitudes teach us anything, it is that holiness begins in the heart.

The words *holy* and *whole* belong to the same family. To be holy involves wholeness. Sin divides and destroys, but holiness unites and builds. Holiness is a basic attribute of God: "God is light; in him there is no darkness at all" (1 John 1:5). When you hunger for holiness, you hunger for God. "My soul thirsts for God!" And to have God in your life means wholeness; He puts everything together. "Through Him all things are held together" (Colossians 1:17 Williams). When the prodigal son hungered for material possessions and thrills, everything fell apart. When he came to himself and returned to his father, everything was made whole again. In fact, what he was looking for in the far country he found right at home.

To be righteous means to be right—right with God, right with self, and right with others. When you hunger and thirst for God, you are causing the inner person to function as God made it to function. Your spiritual senses are exercised and developed (Hebrews 5:14). "Train yourself to be godly" (1 Timothy 4:7). There is a unity to the life of the person whose deepest desire is to know and please God and to enjoy Him. Instead of running from one substitute to another, seeking inner satisfaction, that person says, "All my fountains are in you" (Psalm 87:7). "Lord, to whom shall we go? You have the words of eternal life" (John 6:68).

As the inner person is satisfied with holiness, it becomes increasingly dissatisfied with sin. "Let those that love the Lord hate evil" (Psalm 97:10). To begin with, the mind grows in its recognition of sin. The closer we get to the light, the easier it is to see the defilement. The more we are satisfied with God, the more we are dissatisfied with substitutes, including religious substitutes. The mind recognizes sin, and the heart is repulsed by sin. The dog returns to its vomit, and the sow wallows in the mire, but the sheep has nothing to do with either one. The mind recognizes sin, the heart is repulsed by sin, and the will refuses sin. It is the appreciation of the excellent that motivates the believer to refuse the cheap and defiled.

When you control hunger, you control life. Find out what a person's deep appetites are, provide the satisfaction, and you control that one's life. Dictators and propagandists have followed this principle for centuries. If the appetite is not there, create one. The advertising agencies sell their services for this very purpose. It is unfortunate when our churches create appetites for lesser things—for religious entertainment instead of spiritual food, for multiplied activities instead of spiritual ministries, for sentimental music instead of the spiritual songs of Zion. Having once created the appetite, they must satisfy it, and this plunges our churches into that terrible maelstrom of promotion, celebrities, statistics, and instant results. The sheep need to be led by the quiet waters, but they find themselves drowning in a whirlpool called success.

People who want to master a skill must have a deep desire to do so or they will fail. Perhaps their motives are mixed, but if there is a hunger for achievement, they will have an easier time. Change the hunger and you change the person; control the hunger and you control the person. Jesus Christ wants to create in us a deep hunger for God, a hunger for holiness. It is this hunger that will change and control our lives as we satisfy it in Jesus.

HAPPINESS

It must have come as a surprise to His listeners when Jesus equated holiness and happiness. He promised that they would be blessed if they hungered and thirsted after righteousness. They had seen the Pharisees practice their brand of holiness, and the Pharisees did not seem happy. There seemed to be no touch of blessing in their lives. The people in that day, like people today, equated holy living with misery. Why did they do that?

For one thing, they had the wrong idea of holiness. They thought of it in terms of negatives, for that was all that they saw in the Pharisees. The Pharisees were better known for what they were *against* rather than what they were *for*. Unfortunately, some Christians are that way today. Their Christian experience is a painful bondage instead of a glorious liberty. Jesus enjoyed life, even though life for Him was difficult. He was happy because He was holy. The Pharisees were neither happy nor holy, and Jesus pointed that out to them, so they crucified Him. His joyful, holy life so exposed their brittle piety that He became their enemy. Because the Pharisees had a faulty view of holiness, they robbed themselves of happiness.

But they also had a faulty view of sin, and a person with a faulty view of sin will not know how to find the righteousness that satisfies the inner person. Righteousness for them was a matter of meeting certain external regulations, and sin was simply not obeying those regulations. They never looked deep within their hearts as Paul did when he said, "What a wretched man I am! Who will rescue me from this body of death?" (Romans 7:24). A wrong view of sin and a wrong view of holiness go together. When Isaiah saw the holiness of God, he immediately saw his own sinfulness, and he cried out, "Woe to me! I am ruined!" (Isaiah 6:5). The apostle John once rested upon Jesus' bosom, but when the aged apostle saw the vision of the risen Priest-King, he fell at His feet as though he were dead (Revelation 1:17). The unbeliever cannot understand how Christians can behold the holiness of God, then confess their own helplessness and out of this experience find happiness. But, understand it or not, this is the divine formula: holiness, helplessness, happiness.

We must grow in our love for holiness. No doubt at the beginning of our spiritual walk we seek righteousness in order to avoid pain, the way little children obey so that they might not receive a spanking. This is a negative approach to building character, but it is the best way for a child. We have to begin somewhere. As we grow in grace, we discover that holy living not only avoids chastening but it also brings positive reward. "No good thing does he withhold from those whose walk is blameless" (Psalm 84:11). The danger here, of course, is that we are more concerned with the blessing than the Blesser, and holy living must be the result of a personal relationship. When we discover this truth, we graduate into the third level: We seek holiness in order to please the Father. The result of this experience is to reach an even higher level: We seek a holy life because we love God and want to glorify Him. The Pharisees loved themselves and sought to glorify themselves, and, as Jesus said, they had their reward.

Seeking to please the Father and cultivating a hunger for holiness brings about a remarkable change in our lives: We become more like Him. After all, we are what we eat, and if our food is to do the will of God, then our lives become the will of God. The will of God is not simply something we do; it is something we are. Holiness becomes to us the beauty of God, and we want that beauty for our own lives. You would never have looked at the Pharisees and yearned to have what they had, but if you had watched Jesus come and go among the people, you would have hungered for what He was. The publicans and sinners were attracted by the holiness of Christ; they were repelled by the religious piety of the Pharisees (Luke 15:1–2).

One of the essential differences between mere outward piety and true holiness is that piety makes you conform to a system, whereas true holiness conforms you to Christ and develops your own individuality. The Pharisees were each like the other; the disciples were individual and distinctive. The more we become like Christ, the more we are liberated to become our best selves. Abraham and Moses were both men of God, yet each was different from the other. Spurgeon and Moody were both men of God, deeply taught in the lessons of God's grace, yet neither was like the other one. The "splendor of his holiness" (Psalm 29:2) is not by imitation but by impartation and incarnation. "Christ lives in me" (Galatians 2:20).

HARMONY

How does holiness bring happiness?

If knowing God, enjoying God, and becoming like God is our highest desire, then the fulfilling of that desire will bring us the highest happiness. "They will be filled" is Christ's promise; that word *filled* carries with it a double meaning: "satisfied" and "controlled by." If we hunger and thirst after God's righteousness, then He will satisfy that hunger; and when He has satisfied it, we will discover that our lives are controlled by His righteousness in all that we do. Seeking to become like Him pleases both the Father and us. The higher we climb by His grace on this highway of holiness, the less satisfied we are with the things that make others happy. The disciples had come a long way in their spiritual walk when they could pray, "Lord, show us the Father, and it is enough for us" (John 14:8 NASB).

Holiness brings happiness not only by sparing us the pain of sin and its consequences but also by purifying our hearts and minds and giving us an appetite for the eternal. "And I—in righteousness I will see your face; when I awake, I will be satisfied with seeing your likeness" (Psalm 17:15). As we become more like Christ, we share more of His joy.

Too many Christians believe they can satisfy their hunger for holiness by multiplied activities and special endeavors, when each of these could do more harm than good. It is usually not in the multiplying of activities but in the simplifying of life that we experience the deepest satisfaction in Christ. This does not mean that we necessarily do less; rather, it means that what we do is centered in Christ so that He has the preeminence. "But one thing I do" (Philippians 3:13). "Martha, Martha, you are worried and upset about many things, but only one thing is needed" (Luke 10:41–42). "One thing I ask of the Lord, this is what I seek: that I may dwell in the house of the Lord all the days of my life, to gaze upon the beauty of the Lord and to seek him in his temple" (Psalm 27:4).

Growing in holiness simplifies our lives, unifies our lives, and satisfies our lives. No more of the broken cisterns; we are drinking at the pure river of the water of life. No more of the fleshpots of Egypt; we have the bread of life. The praises of other people fall on deaf ears; we want only the approval of God. The wealth of this world means little to us, for we rejoice in the riches of grace in Christ Jesus.

Growing in holiness, however, does not mean that we lose the good things of this world; rather, it means that we receive them back and enjoy them more. It is God "who richly provides us with everything for our enjoyment" (1 Timothy 6:17). Abraham placed Isaac on the altar and, in the will of God, died to self, but Abraham received him back to enjoy him in a deeper way than ever before. Jesus enjoyed playing with the children, feasting at the table, watching the birds and the lilies, and doing the everyday tasks of life. True holiness (which is wholeness) touches all of life, not merely a part. The Pharisees fasted twice a week and accused Jesus of being a glutton and a drunk. But their fasting was not an exercise in holiness; consequently, their fasting was sin. Our Lord's feasting was in the holy will of God because all of His life was controlled by that will. Holiness always involves *wholeness*—the whole person, the whole of life. "Whether you eat or drink or whatever you do, do it all for the glory of God" (1 Corinthians 10:31). The Pharisee could never be happy because he was not whole and his life was not whole. He was trying to patch his old garment with new cloth, and the seams would not hold. Jesus wore the seamless garment of holiness—wholeness—and walked in the joy of the Lord.

There is no holy living apart from the holy Son of God, the holy Word of God, and the Holy Spirit of God; they go together. The Spirit of God reveals the Son of God through the Word of God. If you have a hunger for holiness, then you will read the Word of God, meditate on it, and make it a vital part of your life. In the Word of God you will see the Son of God, and when you do, the Spirit of God will transform you so that you become more and more like Him. "But we all, with unveiled face beholding as in a mirror the glory of the Lord, are being transformed into the same image from glory to glory, just as from the Lord, the Spirit" (2 Corinthians 3:18 NASB). Moses did not get a shining face by looking at himself; he spent forty days gazing at the glory of the Lord. Stephen looked away from the hateful faces of his persecutors and gazed upon the face of Christ, and his own face radiated the glory of God (Acts 6:15).

There is no escaping the fact that the men and women of God in the Bible and church history dared to reject the comfortable piety of their age and abandon themselves to experience the holiness of God. They hungered and thirsted after righteousness, and God satisfied them. They paid a price, but the reward was worth it. No more could they return to the broken cisterns—even the religious cisterns—once they had drunk deeply of the living waters. The heroes of faith in Hebrews 11 were not persecuted because of their religion but because what they believed so affected the way they behaved that they became a threat to the religious conformists around them. After the Exodus Israel constantly wanted to go back to Egypt. They forgot the slavery; they remembered only the leeks, the onions, and the garlic. But while they were looking back, Moses was looking ahead, and he "persevered because he saw him who is invisible" (Hebrews 11:27). Moses had a different appetite from that of the people, and therefore he had a different ambition. No wonder holy men and women of God have always been persecuted by the religious crowd and utterly rejected by the people of the world. They "faced jeers and flogging, while still others were chained and put in prison. They were stoned; they were sawed in two; they were put to death by the sword. They went about in sheepskins and goatskins, destitute, persecuted and mistreated—

the world was not worthy of them" (Hebrews 11:36–38). And all because they hungered and thirsted after righteousness.

If we are to reign in life and live like kings, we must have God's righteousness, imputed and imparted. God's grace reigns in our lives through righteousness (Romans 5:21). Jesus Christ, our High Priest, belongs to the order of Melchizedek—"king of righteousness." The prodigal son became a slave when he rebelled against his father and lived to please himself. When he returned to his father and submitted to righteousness, he experienced grace and began to live like a king.

All of God's blessings are the by-products of His righteousness. "But seek first his kingdom and his righteousness, and all these things will be given to you as well" (Matthew 6:33). "All these things"—such as food, clothing, shelter, income, husband, wife. When we live for God's rule and God's righteousness in our lives, then we enjoy everything else.

There is no shortcut to happiness or holiness. We must begin with hunger—a hunger for holiness, a deep desire to be more like Christ. God promises to satisfy this hunger, and it is our responsibility to seek to develop this appetite for the righteousness of God. We are what we eat. "Blessed are those who hunger and thirst for righteousness, for they will be filled."

Blessed are the merciful, for they will be shown mercy.
(MATTHEW 5:7)

But the wisdom that comes from heaven is first of all pure;
then peace-loving, considerate, submissive, full of mercy
and good fruit, impartial and sincere.
(JAMES 3:17)

If it is showing mercy, let him do it cheerfully.
(ROMANS 12:8)

Put on therefore, as the elect of God, holy and beloved,
bowels of mercies.
(COLOSSIANS 3:12 KJV)

Which of these three do you think was a neighbor to the man
who fell into the hands of robbers? The expert in the law
replied, "The one who had mercy on him."
(LUKE 10:36–37)

7

THE MERCIFUL

The Roman world did not admire mercy. Romans admired justice, courage, self-control, and wisdom—but not mercy. The philosophers called mercy "a disease of the soul," something to be abhorred and ashamed of if you expected to be a success. Slaves were treated as disposable property, and the position of women and children was far from ideal. If a woman gave birth to a daughter or a sickly son, the father had the option of rejecting the child and having it exposed to die. A temperamental master could, in a fit of anger, maim or even kill a slave. An enemy was an enemy, and the best enemy was a dead enemy.

Jesus Christ and the gospel began to change all of that. Jesus taught and practiced mercy, and He commanded His followers to show mercy. But when Jesus and His followers practiced mercy, it was a revelation of power, not weakness. Instead of being a sickness of the soul, mercy is the health of the Christian experience.

Our world today is not far removed spiritually from the Roman world in which Jesus gave the Beatitudes. People are still treated like things, power is the supreme deity, and financial success is the most important thing in life. How can a person practice mercy in a competitive society? Yet this is exactly what Jesus commands us to do.

GOD'S MERCY

According to theologians, God has two kinds of attributes: absolute and relative. The absolute attributes describe what God is like in Himself, totally apart from His creation. God is love even if there are no human beings around to know about it. God is truth, and God is holy. These are essential characteristics of His being. But when God created humans, He had to "translate" these attributes into His relationship with them, and so we have what theologians call the "relative attributes." Truth becomes faithfulness, holiness becomes justice, and love becomes grace and mercy. Mercy is one of the spiritual bridges God has built so that He can relate to you and me, and mercy is a bridge you and I must build if we are going to relate lovingly to others.

God's mercy and grace grow out of His love. Nobody is saved because God loves him or her, for God loves the whole world. Sinners are saved because of God's grace and mercy, His love in action. It is easy to remember the difference between grace and mercy. God in His grace gives me what I do not deserve. In His mercy He does not give me what I do deserve. In one sense, grace is positive whereas mercy is negative, although this should not be carried too far. "It is of the Lord's mercies that we are not consumed" (Lamentations 3:22 KJV). "The Lord was merciful to [Lot and his family]" (Genesis 19:16). "Lord, have mercy on my son" (Matthew 17:15). It is mercy that pities and grace that pardons.

There are several factors involved in this experience of mercy. It begins with pain; somebody hurts us unjustly, and we must respond to this hurt. If we have no power, then all we can do is give in, but if we have the powers to retaliate, then we must decide what to do. You cannot show mercy unless you have the power to hurt. Suppose the person deserves to be hurt. Suppose the offense against us is so serious that we feel we must teach the offender a lesson. We have the powers to hurt that person back. Should we use them? At this point love enters the picture, not to cancel truth, but to control it. We are hurt; we have the powers and (we believe) the right to hurt the one who hurt us. But because of God's love, we show mercy; we do not give the offender what he or she deserves. This demands faith; we must leave the offender and offense in the hands of God. "Do not take revenge, my friends" (Romans 12:19). What is the result of this painful experience? Growth! We share in the fellowship of his sufferings (Philippians 3:10) and become more like Him.

These, then, are the links in the chain of mercy: pain, power, truth, love, faith, and growth. We suffer because of another's sin, but we choose to use our power for growth instead of retaliation. It is the act of faith that shows the mercy that converts pain into spiritual growth. It is love that makes us want to exercise this faith; it is the Holy Spirit within who gives us this love.

It is an awesome thought that when I show mercy, I am practicing one of the attributes of God. Mercy puts me in the place of God in somebody's life. The Beatitudes begin with the right attitude toward myself—poor in spirit. The next step is a right attitude toward my sin—I mourn. Then, a right attitude toward God's Word—"Blessed are the meek." This creates within me a deep desire for God's righteousness, and He gives it to me when I trust Christ. The first three Beatitudes are preparation for the miracle of the fourth when we, by faith, receive the righteousness of God. And, having received His righteousness, we then begin to be like God: "Blessed are the merciful." "Be imitators of God, therefore, as dearly loved children" (Ephesians 5:1). Having received His divine nature, we begin to manifest His divine attributes, and mercy is one of His attributes.

HUMAN MERCY

Perhaps the best way to understand mercy is to see it in action.

Our first example is in Genesis 14, the story of Abraham's courageous rescue of his nephew Lot. To begin with, Lot had no business in Sodom. If he had been a spiritually minded man, he would have walked with Abraham and obeyed the Lord. But he decided to move into Sodom. When enemy kings attacked Sodom, Lot had to suffer the consequences. He and his family were taken captive, and all their possessions were confiscated. When word got to Abraham, the patriarch immediately gathered his servants and, with the help of God, went to battle and rescued Lot. That was an act of mercy. Abraham could have said, "Well, the young man is stubborn and didn't know when he was well-off. Let him stew in his own juice!" Hadn't Abraham given Lot first choice of the land? Hadn't Lot's choice been a foolish one? Then why rescue him? Because it was the merciful thing to do for a brother (Genesis 14:16). Abraham had the power to hurt Lot and certainly Lot had hurt Abraham, yet in faith and love Abraham chose to show mercy. In the New Testament, Abraham is honored as the great man of faith, and rightly so. But faith plus love equals mercy, and Abraham had all three.

A second example is Joseph. If your brothers treated you the way Joseph's brothers treated him, what would you do to them once they were under your power? They had lied about him, caused him to suffer, and sold him as a slave. Most of them even wanted to kill him! But now the tables were turned: The brothers were bowing before the prime minister of Egypt—Joseph—and he had the power to hurt them. What a temptation! Joseph faced two great temptations in his life, and in both instances he came out victorious. Potiphar's wife tempted him to commit a sin of the flesh, but he fled from her and kept himself pure. His brothers tempted him to commit a sin of the spirit—he could have taken vengeance upon them—but instead he went off and wept and then came back and showed mercy. To be sure, Joseph so dealt with his brothers that he was sure their hearts were changed before he openly forgave them, but even this was an evidence of his mercy. Joseph was neither a prodigal son nor an elder brother; he did not yield to either a sin of the flesh or a sin of the spirit. Instead, he was like Jesus Christ, the Son of God, who prayed, "Father, forgive them; for they do not know not what they are doing" (Luke 23:34).

Our third example of true mercy is David, the man after God's own heart—and therefore the man who revealed God's own heart. David was the true anointed king of Israel, even though Saul was still exercising power to persecute David and his men. On two occasions David had Saul in his power and could have killed him (1 Samuel 24, 26), but he refused to do so. Instead, he showed mercy. Some of David's men wanted him to kill their enemy; they argued that God had brought Saul into their power. But David knew that his real power was not in killing but in showing mercy. In fact, when Saul finally was killed, David sang a lamentation and made no mention whatsoever of Saul's hatred toward him (2 Samuel 1:17–27). "Your glory, O Israel, lies slain on your heights. How the mighty have fallen!" (v. 19).

In each of these instances, there were both pain and the power to retaliate. But there was also "faith expressing itself through love" (Galatians 5:6), and this resulted in mercy. The act of mercy put the one showing mercy on the throne, for it was Abraham who was in control, not Lot; it was Joseph and David who reigned in life, not their persecutors. We might add that Joseph's experience of mercy made life happier and easier for his brothers, and they reigned in life with him. When you show mercy, it not only helps you to grow and reign, but it also helps others. If, like Saul, others refuse the mercy that you offer, then God will judge them. If, like Joseph's brothers, they accept mercy, God will bless them. The choice is theirs, not ours.

MERCY AND THE CROSS

The greatest example of one showing mercy is, of course, the Lord Jesus Christ. How simple it would have been for Him to answer His enemies with deeds of judgmental power instead of words of grace. The intensity of their opposition increased the closer He came to Calvary, and yet the strength of His mercy matched the intensity of their hatred. It is not that in His mercy He refused to expose His enemies' sins; the sermon in Mathew 23 is proof enough that mercy does not sweep the dust under the rug. When the chief priests and rulers had Him arrested, they gave Him in that act a glorious opportunity to avenge Himself. Had He done so, nobody would have criticized Him. Instead, He willingly submitted to the mob and rebuked His impetuous disciple. "Do you think I cannot call on my Father, and he will at once put at my disposal more than twelve legions of angels?" (Matthew 26:53).

We see in Jesus Christ the fulfillment of Psalm 85:10 (KJV): "Mercy and truth are met together; righteousness and peace have kissed each other." He knew and even exposed the truth about sinners, and yet He showed mercy to them. The feeble mercy that cultured people show to each other is usually based on ignorance or deception. "If we knew all we would forgive all," is their motto. Or, "I am just as sinful as you are, so I will show mercy to you because you will show mercy to me." Although it is better than nothing, the humanistic approach to mercy falls far short of the divine ideal.

Jesus showed mercy, yet He certainly could not plead either ignorance or sin. Jesus "did not need man's testimony about man, for he knew what was in a man" (John 2:25). "Can any of you prove me guilty of sin?" (John 8:46). He was able to show mercy because of His work on the cross. It was there that mercy and truth met together and righteousness and peace kissed each other. His death at Calvary was a testimony to the truth that we are sinners, and yet it was also a triumph over sin in that it opened up the fountains of the mercy of God. There is a "judgment without mercy" (James 2:13), but it is not at Calvary. On the cross, there was judgment *with* mercy.

This fact suggests that you and I, if we are not discerning, can practice a kind of counterfeit mercy that denies truth and righteousness and does not lead to peace. Perhaps this is the kind of mercy that David showed Absalom when he excused Absalom for killing his brother, Amnon, thus sowing the seeds of rebellion in the boy's heart. David's mourning over Absalom's death is one of the most poignant scenes in all literature, but nothing could have changed Absalom's character, let alone his tragic destiny. Whenever mercy is extended, it must be on the basis of truth, and David's mercy toward his son was not on that basis. There is no record that Absalom ever repented (that is where the truth comes in) or that David ever encouraged him to repent (that is where righteousness comes in). The whole transaction was shallow and sentimental, not spiritual. We have too many transactions of the same tragic character in our churches today.

Another example of counterfeit mercy is Ahab's treatment of Ben-Hadad, a rival king (1 Kings 20:32). Ordered to slay the enemy king, Ahab spared him in what seemed to be a great act of mercy. But mercy and truth did not meet that day, and the result was not righteousness or peace. The result was sin and war. Ahab spared his enemy in order to feed his own ego and become a great hero. He gave no thought to the will or glory of God.

To extend mercy means to withhold judgment. Mercy means that God does not give us what we deserve. But there can be no true mercy apart from justice; somebody simply has to pay the price for sin. This is where the cross comes in: "He himself bore our sins in his body on the tree" (1 Peter 2:24). God forgives us and shows us mercy on the basis of His Son's sacrifice, and we show mercy to others on that same basis. Were it not for Calvary, mercy and truth could never meet together, and righteousness and peace would never result.

"Father, forgive them, for they do not know what they are doing" (Luke 23:34). Of what were they ignorant? Of the person against whom they were sinning, for one thing. "Now brothers, I know that you acted in ignorance, as did your leaders" (Acts 3:17). They were also ignorant of the enormity of their sin. They were rejecting God and making Him suffer! Ignorance does not remove guilt, but it could mitigate the sentence. Our Lord's prayer for the nation did not automatically result in the personal forgiveness of all those who had been involved in His arrest and crucifixion. But it did postpone God's judgment and give the nation another opportunity to repent. That is mercy.

It is the cross that makes mercy available to us and through us. We must never extend mercy on the basis of our own "spirituality" but rather on the basis of His finished sacrifice. If the mercy we show bypasses the cross, then it also bypasses truth and righteousness, and it can never lead to peace. "But the wisdom that comes from heaven is first of all pure; then peace-loving" (James 3:17). "Peace at any price" is never a basis for mercy. "Making peace through his blood, shed on the cross" (Colossians 1:20) is the only true basis for mercy. How can we tell the one from the other in actual practice? Counterfeit mercy always inflates the ego of believers, but true mercy humbles them and gives God the glory.

EXPERIENCING MERCY

You cannot extend mercy until you have received it. Mercy is not a quality natural to humans; it must be received as a gift from God. "He saved us, not because of righteous things we had done, but because of his mercy" (Titus 3:5). But the receiving of mercy cannot be a mere commercial transaction between God and me; I must experience it in my heart. The problem with the unmerciful servant in Christ's parable (Matthew 18:21–35) was that he looked upon the king's mercy as something that could have been earned if only there had been time enough to work. "Lord, have patience with me, and I will pay you all!" The man was never really broken by the debt of his sins, and therefore his attitude was that of a prankster who had been let off the hook and not of a rebel who had been delivered from death. He received mercy in a commercial manner; he did not experience mercy in a spiritual manner. For this reason he was unable to extend mercy to his fellow worker, who owed him a paltry sum when compared with his own debt.

The need to experience mercy may help to explain the Lord's Supper. Most of us want to forget the death of a loved one, yet Jesus wants us to remember His death. Why? In coming to the Lord's Supper, we must first examine ourselves (1 Corinthians 11:28), and that means to be confronted with mercy and truth. We must confess the truth about ourselves and then claim His mercy in forgiveness. We do not come to the Lord's Table to remember our sins; we come to remember Christ. But we cannot eat or drink in a worthy manner if we do not tell the truth to God and ourselves. The broken bread and the cup remind us of the mercy of God.

"Remember that you were slaves in Egypt and the Lord your God redeemed you" (Deuteronomy 15:15). The Christian never says with the worldly sentimentalist, "I am a sinner; therefore, I can show mercy to you." Rather, the Christian says, "I am a *forgiven* sinner, and because I have experienced mercy and truth at Calvary, I can extend mercy to you." Sins committed can never be the fountain for mercy. It is when sins are forgiven that "mercy and truth are met together."

But salvation is only the beginning; there must also be submission. Have you ever noticed that Romans 12 begins with surrender and ends with "Do not take revenge, my friends" (v. 19)? Being a "living sacrifice" means living the sacrifice of Christ. It was while their persecutors were crucifying Him that He prayed, "Father, forgive them for they do not know what they are doing." Romans 12 does not stop with verse 2! It goes on to say, "Bless those who persecute you; bless and do not curse . . . Do not repay anyone evil for evil . . . Do not take revenge, my friends . . . Do not be not overcome by evil, but overcome evil with good" (Romans 12:14, 17, 19, 21). David knew that it was not his privilege to exercise vengeance, so he left Saul in the hands of God. David showed mercy. Because he was submissive to the will of God, he was able to "leave room for" the wrath of God (Romans 12:19).

Besides salvation and submission, there is a third essential that we must possess if we are going to extend mercy, and that is suffering. When mercy and truth meet together, the result has to be suffering. Those extending mercy suffer because they experience the hurt caused by their enemy, and those receiving mercy suffer as they realize what they have done and repent of their sin. Whenever you are dealing with sin, there is going to be pain. But the experience of mercy heals the wounds and turns the suffering into joy.

This principle is illustrated in John 8, where the Pharisees burst into our Lord's morning message and confront Him with the woman taken in the act of adultery. The record indicates that there are several ways to deal with sin. There is the way of Moses, the way of the law. "In the Law Moses commanded us to stone such women" (John 8:5). Law can never cleanse; it can only condemn. It cannot give power to keep from sinning; it can only inflict judgment after sin has been committed. Jesus rejected that way.

A second way to deal with sin is the human way: Find the sinner, expose the sinner, and even use the sinner to accomplish your own selfish purposes—in other words, play God. Jesus dealt with this egotistical approach in one simple sentence: "If any one of you is without sin, let him be the first to throw a stone at her" (John 8:7).

If Moses' way is rejected, and if the human way is not accepted, then what is left? The Master's way. "'Then neither do I condemn you,' Jesus declared. 'Go now and leave your life of sin'" (John 8:11). Notice that Jesus did not deny the fact of sin. He knew the woman was a sinner, and she knew that she was a sinner. But mercy and truth met together that morning, and the result was a forgiven sinner. But think of what that forgiveness cost Jesus. Think of how His holy soul was pained by the woman's sin and by the self-righteous judgment of the religious leaders. And think of the suffering He would endure on the cross to make her cleansing possible. There can be no mercy without suffering, no pardon without pain.

Vindictive, defensive Christians are protecting themselves; merciful Christians are making themselves vulnerable. In the parable of the Good Samaritan, the priest and the Levite hurried past the half-dead traveler and saved themselves suffering and danger. (After all, those same robbers might still be around!) But the Good Samaritan made himself vulnerable; he deliberately exposed himself to suffering so that he might show mercy and escape suffering. But the suffering we experience is not destructive; it is the fellowship of his sufferings (Philippians 3:10). Some of David's greatest psalms came out of his painful experiences with Saul and Absalom. Some of your greatest songs will be born the same way.

EXTENDING MERCY TO OTHERS

"Blessed are the merciful, for they will be shown mercy." What does it mean to obtain mercy? Certainly it does not mean that we *earn* mercy because we *extend* mercy, for such an idea is foreign to the Word of God. By its very definition, mercy cannot be earned any more than grace can be earned. The Beatitude is saying that when you experience and share mercy, then your heart is in such a condition that you can receive more mercy to share with others. In other words, Jesus is not asking us to be merciful occasionally; He is asking us to be constant channels of mercy. "Give, and it will be given to you" (Luke 6:38). By extending mercy, we open our hearts to receive mercy; having received, we can share again and again.

Christians are surrounded by mercy. We can say, "Surely goodness and mercy shall follow me all the days of my life" (Psalm 23:6 KJV). When we look ahead, we remember the words of Jude 21—"Wait for the mercy of our Lord Jesus Christ to bring you to eternal life." As we begin each new day, we can say, "It is of the Lord's mercies that we are not consumed, because his compassions fail not. They are new every morning: great is thy faithfulness" (Lamentations 3:22–23 KJV).

It is a basic fact of theology that God responds to us on the basis of the condition of the heart. "With the merciful You will show Yourself merciful; With a blameless man You will show Yourself blameless; With the pure You will show Yourself pure; And with the devious You will show Yourself shrewd" (Psalm 18:25–26 NKJV). Jacob was a schemer and a fighter, so God had to wrestle with him and break him before He could bless him. Peter was an impetuous self-sufficient man, so Jesus had to let him plunge into denial and defeat before He could make him a success. When once we begin to cultivate one of the spiritual graces, God always provides more. When we show mercy, He gives mercy, and thus we have more mercy to show.

When we Christians show mercy, we experience liberation. We are set free from grudges that drain the strength and unsettle the mind. The unmerciful servant in the parable (Matthew 18:21–35) put himself and his family into prison because he could not forgive a friend. The most miserable prison in the world is the prison we make for ourselves when we refuse to show mercy. Our thoughts become shackled, our emotions are chained, and the will is almost paralyzed. But when we show mercy, all of those bonds are broken, and we enter into a joyful liberty that frees us to share God's love with others. This blessing of freedom is one way that we receive mercy as we show mercy. It is a blessed by-product of obeying God.

You can be sure that there will always be opportunities to show mercy. We never grow out of this privilege. But what a glorious experience it is! How thrilling it is to go through life sharing God's mercy and not having to judge people to see if they are "worthy" of what we have to offer. We stop looking at the externals and begin to see people through the merciful eyes of Christ. Every Christian we meet is a person in whom Jesus lives; every lost soul we meet is a person for whom Jesus died. In both cases, we have candidates for God's mercy.

The only way God could get His mercy to this world was through His Son. The Son of God had to become flesh before mercy and truth could meet together. It is the same today; mercy in the abstract means nothing—it must always be incarnate in human flesh. The evasive lawyer wanted Jesus to discuss the abstract question of "Who is my neighbor?" But Jesus forced him to see one half-dead stranger at the side of the road and one hated alien who showed mercy to that stranger. The world cannot see mercy apart from the people who experience it and share it.

You and I are to be those people.

Blessed are the pure in heart, for they will see God.
(MATTHEW 5:8)

*The eye is the lamp of the body. If your eyes are good,
your whole body will be full of light. But if your eyes are bad,
your whole body will be full of darkness. If then the
light within you is darkness, how great is that darkness!*
(MATTHEW 6:22–23)

*No one has ever seen God, but God the One and Only,
who is at the Father's side, has made him known.*
(JOHN 1:18)

*O God, you are my God, earnestly I seek you . . .
I have seen you in the sanctuary and
beheld your power and your glory.*
(PSALM 63:1–2)

They will see his face.
(REVELATION 22:4)

8

THE PURE IN HEART

At some point in life, each of us must decide what is our highest joy, for the thing that delights us directs us. Generally speaking, children find their delight in what they *have*; youths in what they *do*; and adults in what they *are*. The first live for possessions, the second for experiences, and the third for character. We do not condemn children or youths for living as they do because they haven't reached maturity, but we would certainly wonder at an adult who lived on those lower levels. The adult should know that possessions and experiences are empty apart from character. What we are determines how much we enjoy what we have and what we do.

All people have an outlook on life; they are seeking their highest joy. Outlook determines outcome. Abraham lifted up his eyes and saw the stars and became the friend of God by faith. Lot lifted up his eyes and saw Sodom and became the friend of the world. Abraham inherited the city prepared for him by God, the city he had been seeking (Hebrews 11:13–16), but Lot lost everything when Sodom went up in smoke.

If life is to be rich and meaningful, then our joys must be the highest possible, and Jesus tells us that the highest joy possible is to see God.

WHAT IS THE HEART?

Let's begin with the word *heart*—"Blessed are the pure in heart, for they will see God." Biblical psychology is not always as scientifically precise as we would like it to be. Paul writes about our "whole spirit, soul and body" (1 Thessalonians 5:23), and theologians suggest that the spirit is God-consciousness, the soul is self-consciousness, and the body is world-consciousness. Some students further suggest that the soul includes the God-given functions of intellect, emotion, and will. These are convenient categories, but they may not always be consistent. Jesus tells us that the greatest commandment is to love God with all your heart, soul, mind, and strength, indicating *four* functions of personality.

Sometimes the Bible uses the word *heart* to indicate the emotions. "Do not let your hearts be troubled" (John 14:1). "This can be nothing but sadness of heart" (Nehemiah 2:2). But the heart can also refer to the intellect. "Why do you reason about these things in your hearts?" (Mark 2:8 NKJV). Hebrews 4:12 (KJV) states that the Word of God is a "discerner of the thoughts and intents of the heart." The heart also indicates the volitional function, the will. "But Daniel purposed in his heart that he would not defile himself" (Daniel 1:8 KJV). Jesus admonished His disciples, "Therefore settle it in your hearts not to meditate beforehand on what you will answer" (Luke 21:14 NKJV).

Putting it all together, you get the impression that *heart* simply means the inner person with its many functions. This is the "master control" area of life. "Above all else, guard your heart, for it is the wellspring of life" (Proverbs 4:23). It is here that salvation is experienced: "That if you shall confess with your mouth, 'Jesus as Lord,' and believe in your heart that God raised him from the dead, you will be saved" (Romans 10:9). The Pharisees tried to please God, but they ignored the heart and majored on outward actions. "These people honor me with their lips," said Jesus, "but their hearts are far from me" (Matthew 15:8).

The heart, of course, is the source of all our trouble. We are prone to blame people and circumstances, and even God, for the wrong things that we do, but the heart is really the culprit. "The heart is deceitful above all things and beyond cure. Who can understand it?" (Jeremiah 17:9). Neither time nor experience has changed the human heart. God's indictment before the flood is just as valid today: "The Lord saw how great man's wickedness on the earth had become, and that every inclination of the thoughts of his heart was only evil all the time" (Genesis 6:5). Jesus spells it out in greater detail: "For out of the heart come evil thoughts, murder, adultery, sexual immorality, theft, false testimony, slander" (Matthew 15:19). The first step toward seeing God is admitting that my heart is sinful and that I cannot see God unless my heart is changed.

Can the heart be changed? "I will give them a heart to know me, that I am the Lord" (Jeremiah 24:7). "'This is the covenant I will make with them after that time, says the Lord. I will put my laws in their hearts, and I will write them on their minds.' Then he adds: 'Their sins and lawless acts I will remember no more'" (Hebrews 10:16–17). Jesus called this experience being "born again" or "born from above" (John 3:1–7), and Peter described it as becoming "partakers of the divine nature" (2 Peter 1:4 KJV). People are not changed from the outside in; they must be changed from the inside out.

The two kings, David and Saul, illustrate this truth. When God called Saul, "God changed Saul's heart" (1 Samuel 10:9), and the beginning of his reign was successful. But then he disobeyed God in failing to wait for Samuel and in acting as the priest, and that was the end of his reign. "But now your kingdom will not endure," Samuel announced, "the Lord has sought out a man *after his own heart*" (1 Samuel 13:14, italics added). Why? "The Lord looks at the heart" (1 Samuel 16:7). David was that man after God's own heart, not because he was sinless but because his heart was single. Saul was a double-minded man. He tried to fear the people and fear the Lord at the same time, and it could not be done. Saul worried about the outward appearance: "Please honor me before the elders of my people and before Israel" (1 Samuel 15:30). David sought no honor for himself but only for God. "Let my enemy pursue and overtake me," David prays in Psalm 7:5. "Let him trample my life to the ground and make me sleep in the dust." He closes that prayer with his desire that God alone might be glorified: "I will give thanks to the Lord because of his righteousness and will sing praise to the name of the Lord Most High" (Psalm 7:17).

You cannot read the Psalms without learning that David cultivated his heart, the inner person. "I will praise you, O Lord, with all my heart" (Psalm 9:1). "May the words of my mouth and the meditation of my heart be pleasing in your sight, O Lord, my Rock and my Redeemer" (Psalm 19:14). "Test me, O Lord, and try me; examine my heart and my mind" (Psalm 26:2). "My heart says of you, 'Seek his face!' Your face, Lord, I will seek" (Psalm 27:8). "My heart is stirred by a noble theme as I recite my verses for the king" (Psalm 45:1). (Did not Jesus say, "Out of the overflow of the heart the mouth speaks" [Matthew 12:34]?) Psalm 57 records David's experiences in the cave when he was hiding from Saul, and twice he stated the desire of his heart: "Be exalted, O God, above the heavens; let your glory be over all the earth" (vv. 5, 11).

What was David's secret? "My heart is steadfast, O God, my heart is steadfast; I will sing and make music" (Psalm 57:7). Saul's heart was not steadfast; it was divided and unstable. "A double-minded man [is] unstable in all he does" (James 1:8). Saul set his heart on receiving honor before the people, and he lost both that and the honor that comes only from God. David set his heart on God and sought to honor Him, and God honored him in a singular way. When the Lord told David that He would build him a house and give him a throne forever (a promise that Messiah would come from David's line), the king was overwhelmed. Like a child, David used his own name as he spoke to God: "What more can David say to you for honoring your servant? For you know your servant" (1 Chronicles 17:18).

The highest joy of humanity comes from cultivating the deepest part of humanity, the heart. When the heart is pure, then the vision is clear, and a person will see God.

WHAT IS A PURE HEART?

The word that is translated *pure* has two basic meanings: "clean" and "unmixed." Our English word *cathartic* comes from this Greek word. A cathartic is an agent a doctor uses to cleanse the physical system. A psychiatrist also uses catharsis on the emotional level to "cleanse" the patient of hostilities and other destructive attitudes. There is also a spiritual catharsis, a cleansing of the inner person. "He purifies their hearts by faith" (Acts 15:9) is one example. "The blood of Jesus, his Son, purifies us from all sin" (1 John 1:7) is another.

But the word as it is used in this Beatitude takes the second meaning, for being "pure in heart" involves being *unmixed* as well as being clean. Milk that is pure is not adulterated with water. Gold with the dross removed is pure gold. Wheat with the chaff removed is pure wheat. The basic idea is that of integrity, singleness of heart, as opposed to duplicity, a double heart, a divided heart. When God cleanses sinners and makes them His children, He does more than merely wash away sin. He puts within them a new heart that wants to focus wholly on God. "I will give them singleness of heart and action, so that they will always fear me for their own good and the good of their children after them" (Jeremiah 32:39). This is spiritual and moral integrity.

It was this integrity that made David a successful king, and it was the lack of this integrity that corrupted and defeated Saul. God rejected Saul's kingship, but "He chose David his servant and took him from the sheep pens . . . And David shepherded them with integrity of heart; with skillful hands he led them" (Psalm 78:70, 72). No matter how skillful the hands may be, if the heart is divided, the work will be destroyed. Samuel Johnson stated it beautifully: "Integrity without knowledge is weak and useless, and knowledge without integrity is dangerous and dreadful." Peter illustrates the first and Judas the second. Peter loved Jesus Christ and boasted that he would die for him; he had integrity but not knowledge. Judas knew where the Lord was, where He would pray and what He could do, but he lacked integrity and used his knowledge to destroy himself and others.

Integrity of heart was David's passionate concern, as is witnessed by many statements in the Psalms. "Judge me, O Lord, according to my righteousness, according to my integrity, O Most High" (Psalm 7:8). "May integrity and uprightness protect me, because my hope is in you" (Psalm 25:21). "Vindicate me, O Lord, for I have led a blameless life . . . But I lead a blameless life" (Psalm 26:1, 11). "In my integrity you uphold me and set me in your presence forever" (Psalm 41:12). That last verse is perhaps the closest thing to this Beatitude that you will find in the Psalms; David had a pure heart, and he saw the face of God.

Jesus illustrates this singleness of heart in Matthew 6:19–23, when He talks about the eye. This is in the section of the Sermon on the Mount dealing with our relationship to wealth, and He is warning us against being double-minded, trying to serve both God and money. "The eye is the lamp of the body. If your eyes are good, your whole body will be full of light. But if your eyes are bad, your whole body will be full of darkness. If then the light within you is darkness, how great is that darkness!" (Matthew 6:22–23). After illustrating this truth by means of the human body, Jesus then illustrates it again by means of human relationships. "No one can serve two masters" (Matthew 6:24). Jesus is speaking here about singleness of devotion, desire, and direction. Psalm 86:11 explains it: "Teach me your way, O Lord, and I will walk in your truth; give me an undivided heart, that I may fear your name." No person can ever hope to see God whose heart is divided between the Lord and the world.

Our relationship with God must be based on love. For our hearts to love anything other than God is to commit spiritual adultery. "You adulterous people, don't you know that friendship with the world is hatred toward God? Anyone who chooses to be a friend of the world becomes an enemy of God" (James 4:4). Because people are at war with God, they are at war with each other. "Saul became still more afraid of [David], and he remained his enemy the rest of his days" (1 Samuel 18:29). The only cure for spiritual adultery is, "Come near to God and he will come near to you. Wash your hands, you sinners, and purify your hearts, you double-minded" (James 4:8). "Love the Lord your God with *all* your heart" (Matthew 22:37, italics added). David did not have a sinless heart, but he did have a single heart, and that made him a man after God's own heart. "I have found David son of Jesse a man after my own heart; he will do everything I want him to do" (Acts 13:22). This verse brings out the contrasts between Saul and David. Saul talked about God's will, but David fulfilled it. Saul wanted his own will, but David wanted God's will. And Saul obeyed only part of God's will, whereas David fulfilled all of it.

How do we maintain this priceless integrity of heart? By being utterly honest with God, others, and ourselves and by seeking to honor God alone. When you read about the life of David, you see a man who sought to live openly and honestly. Twice in his life David resorted to duplicity, and in both instances he got into trouble. The first occurred when David fled to Gath and tried to escape Saul's sword by joining the ranks of the enemy. (Gath was originally the home of Goliath, you will recall.) It became clear that David was no safer in Gath than he was in Judah, so he "pretended to be insane in their presence; and while he was in their hands he acted like a madman, making marks on the doors of the gate and letting saliva run down his beard" (1 Samuel 21:13). This masquerade enabled David to escape, and one result of this experience was the conviction that faith in God alone is the secret of God's protection. David records this conviction in Psalm 34. Duplicity led David almost to death. He fled to the cave of Adullam, and there he wrote Psalm 57 and cried out: "My heart is steadfast, O God, my heart is steadfast" (v. 7). No more duplicity.

David's second masquerade was following the sin with Bathsheba, when he pretended to honor her husband, Uriah. His ruse did not work, and he resorted to outright murder. Psalm 51 is the record of that experience, and once again the integrity of the inner person comes to the fore. "Surely you desire truth in the inner parts" (v. 6). "Create in me a pure heart, O God, and renew a right [steadfast, established] spirit within me" (v. 10). Certainly David had sinned against Bathsheba and Uriah, but when he considered his sin in relationship to the integrity of his heart, he had to pray,

"Against you, you only, have I sinned and done what is evil in your sight" (v. 4).

Saul's life, however, was one masquerade after another, climaxing in that visit to the witch's cave. "Saul disguised himself," announces the historian (1 Samuel 28:8), and from the human point of view, this was true. But from the spiritual point of view Saul did not disguise himself. He revealed himself. In the integrity of his heart, David had fled to a cave and there found God's help. In the duplicity of his heart, Saul fled to a witch and discovered that God had forsaken him and the masquerade was over.

It is instructive to contrast the death of David and the death of Saul, the one resting confidently and directing the affairs of his kingdom up to the very end and the other staggering out into the darkness of defeat and having no control over himself or his kingdom. Saul's last actions are identified with night: "Saul disguised himself, putting on other clothes, and at night he and two men went to the woman . . . That same night they got up and left" (1 Samuel 28:8, 25). Like Saul centuries earlier, Judas went out, "and it was night" (John 13:30). But David's last days are identified with light. "Now these are the last words of David . . . 'When one rules over men in righteousness, when he rules in the fear of God, he is like the light of morning at sunrise on a cloudless morning, like the brightness after rain that brings the grass from the earth'"(2 Samuel 23:1, 3–4).

When you read David's psalms, you realize that he was utterly honest before God. He never prayed anything that he did not mean. If he was afraid or sick or discouraged, he admitted it. Psalm 142 is one of his "cave songs," and in it he says, "I pour out my complaint before him; before him I tell my trouble. When my spirit grows faint within me, it is you who know my way. In the path where I walk men have hidden a snare for me" (vv. 2–3). Imagine complaining to God!

"Hear me and answer me," David cries in Psalm 55:2. "My thoughts trouble me and I am distraught." He was honest with God in his living and in his praying, and this maintained his integrity. He was a man after God's own heart.

Those who, like Pharisees, pretend to be holy and try to serve two masters eventually become shallow and hollow. Theirs is a surface religion that never reaches the heart. They have to use so much energy acting out a part that they have no strength left to live. There is no substitute for integrity. "Blessed are the pure in heart."

HOW DO WE SEE GOD?

"For they shall see God." This is the highest blessing possible for humans, for when we see God, we see Him who is (as the theologians put it) "the Source, Support, and End of all things." Since nothing is higher than God, then seeing God must be the highest joy that we can experience. It was this joy that motivated and excited men and women in Bible times and also inspired the great saints of church history. Moses prayed, "Now show me your glory" (Exodus 33:18). David wrote his heart's desire in Psalm 42:1–2: "As the deer pants for streams of water, so my soul pants for you, O God. My soul thirsts for God, for the living God. When can I go and meet with God?" Phillip said to Jesus, "Show us the Father, and it is enough for us" (John 14:8 NASB). Of course it was for this purpose that Jesus came, that He might reveal God to us. "Anyone who has seen me has seen the Father" (John 14:9).

Why do we seem to have so little of this hunger for God in the church today? We are not lacking in programs or people, activities or "results"; we are lacking in a vision of God or even a desire for such a vision. The men and women God has used in past days have been characterized by a deep hunger to see God and know Him intimately. They have echoed the prayer of David, "O God, you are my God, earnestly I seek you; my soul thirsts for you, my body longs for you, in a dry and weary land where there is no water. I have seen you in the sanctuary and beheld your power and your glory" (Psalm 63:1–2). If Isaiah's experience is any pattern, it would seem that seeing God is a condition for serving God. "In the year that king Uzziah died, I saw the Lord seated on a throne, high and exalted, and the train of his robe filled the temple" (Isaiah 6:1). This was also Paul's experience: He saw a light, and then he saw the Lord.

There is a sense, of course, in which God cannot be seen. "No one has ever seen God " (John 1:18). Even Moses was unable to look upon God in His very essence. "But," the Lord told him, "you cannot see my face, for no one may see me and live" (Exodus 33:20). Paul, who visited the third heaven, described God as the one "who alone is immortal and who lives in unapproachable light, whom no one has seen or can see" (1 Timothy 6:16). Just as the human eye is blinded—and possibly destroyed—by gazing at the full light of the sun, so the spiritual eye cannot behold God in His fullness. No wonder Moses hid his face at the burning bush, "for he was afraid to look upon God" (Exodus 3:6 KJV).

We need that sense of respect today, for too many of God's people evidence a flippant familiarity with God that is not only disrespectful but also downright disgusting. They know God in a secondhand way, but they want us to believe they are among His intimates. They have not yet had the deep experience of Job: "My ears had heard of you but now my eyes have seen you. Therefore I despise myself and repent in dust and ashes" (Job 42:5–6). The apostle John, an intimate friend of Jesus, had a similar experience:

"When I saw him, I fell at his feet as though dead" (Revelation 1:17).

No, God in His essence cannot be seen. How, then, do we see God? When people's hearts are pure, then their eyes are opened to the vision of God wherever He may appear. To be sure, ultimately the children of God will in heaven "see his face" (Revelation 22:4). But it is not this final "beatific vision" of the saints and mystics that this Beatitude is talking about. Jesus is promising us the vision of God here and now. It is a basic principle that we see what we love, so if our hearts are united to fear and love God, then we will see God. We will live in a world that is filled with God.

To begin with, we will see God in His creation. "The heavens declare the glory of God; the skies proclaim the work of his hands"(Psalm 19:1). The Psalms are filled with expressions of joy and wonder as the writer looked at God's world and saw God Himself. In Psalm 29, for example, David watched a storm as it swept over the mountains, but he did not simply see a storm. He saw God. The thunder was the voice of the Lord, and the rushing waters upheld the throne of the Lord. Instead of showing fear as he saw the trees breaking under the wind and the rivers rising, David shouted with confidence, "The Lord sits enthroned over the flood; the Lord is enthroned as King forever" (Psalm 29:10). Because David had a pure heart, he saw God in the stars and in the storms, and he enjoyed living in God's world.

The Lord Jesus had the same vision of God. He saw the providence of God in the fall of the sparrow and the generosity of God in the beauty of the lily. He watched a farmer sow his seed, and in that he saw the Word of God planted in people's hearts. When the sun came up Jesus beheld the grace of God: "He causes his sun to rise on the evil and the good" (Matthew 5:45). Likewise, the rain reminded Him that the Father "sends rain on the righteous and the unrighteous" (Matthew 5:45). For Jesus, nature was alive with God. Not a nebulous Something, a First Cause, or a Prime Mover—but a heavenly Father. "This is my Father's world!"

True, sin has marred creation, and with sin comes sorrow and death. "For we know that the whole creation groans and suffers the pains of childbirth together until now" (Romans 8:22 NASB). But in spite of what sin has done and what sinners are now doing, this is still God's creation, and the saint who has a pure heart clearly sees His fingerprints and footprints. Whenever I become disgusted at the civilization humanity has built, I look deeply into the creation God has built; I read Psalm 104 and give thanks.

We see God in creation, but we also see God in circumstances. In Psalms 105 and 106, for example, the writer saw the hand of God in the history of His people. A. T. Pierson used to say, "History is His story"—and he was right. When Matthew wrote his gospel, he used the word *fulfilled* at least a dozen times, showing us that the events in the life of Christ were controlled by the hand of God. His birth was the fulfillment of Isaiah 7:14. His flight to Egypt fulfilled Hosea 11:1. His growing up in Nazareth fulfilled the promise in the prophets, "He shall be called a Nazarene" (a rejected one). Our Lord's miracles of healing fulfilled Isaiah 53:4. Over and over in the gospel of Matthew we are told that our Lord's early life was a plan from God. And if you and I are in the will of God—if our hearts are single—we too shall see God in the circumstances of life. This was Paul's conviction when he wrote Romans 8:28: "And we know that in all things God works for the good of those who love him, who have been called according to his purpose."

Psalm 23 makes clear that David saw God in the circumstances of his life. Life was not a series of accidents; it was a series of appointments. The Shepherd was in control. Even when David strayed and circumstances were painful, he still saw the Shepherd restoring him and refreshing him. When David looked back he saw God: "Surely goodness and love will follow me all the days of my life"; and when he looked ahead he saw God: "I will dwell in the house of the Lord forever" (Psalm 23:6). Even when going through the dark valley David saw God: "For you are with me." It is significant that in verse 4 David changes from the third person *he* to the second person *you*.

We see God not only in the circumstances of our own lives but also in the march of events in the world. Thoreau was once asked if he wanted to read the newspaper, and he replied that he had read one once. "Blessed are they who never read a newspaper," wrote Thoreau, "for they shall see Nature, and, through her, God." But why sacrifice one for the other? I believe it was John Wesley who said that he read the newspaper to see how God was ruling in His world. There is no such thing as secular and sacred to the person with a pure heart and a single eye. "Who can proclaim the mighty acts of the Lord?" asks the writer of Psalm 106:2, whose eye penetrated deep into the mysteries of God's ways in the world. Nature and life are windows through which we should see God, but if we lack that integrity of heart they become mirrors in which we see only ourselves. Jesus taught this in His parable of the foolish farmer (Luke 12:13–21). In his bumper crop and sudden wealth, the farmer did not see God; he saw only himself. Count the eleven personal pronouns in the farmer's soliloquy and note the repetition of "I will." This man was not pure in heart. He did not see God; he saw only himself.

The pure in heart see God in creation and circumstances and also in His Word. Unlike any other book, the Bible demands preparation of heart if its message is to be understood. As F. W.

Robertson put it, "Obedience is the organ of spiritual knowledge." He finds his basis for this statement in John 7:17: "If anyone is willing to do His will, he will know of the teaching, whether it is of God or whether I speak from Myself" (NASB). We do not understand, then obey: That is instruction. We obey by faith, and then we understand. That is illumination. Double-minded people will never see God in the Bible. They may be book-taught, but they will never be God-taught. Their minds may grasp facts, but their hearts will never lay hold of truths. The Pharisees knew the traditions of the fathers and the opinions of the scholars, but they did not know God. And He was right there in their midst! Bible study is good and important, but Bible knowledge should lead to a deeper knowledge of God. "You search the Scriptures because you think that in them you have eternal life; it is these that testify about Me" (John 5:39 NASB).

THE WIDER VISION

The experience of seeing God through the eyes of the heart is not a momentary thing; it is constant and growing. "But we all, with unveiled face beholding as in a mirror the glory of the Lord, are being transformed into the same image, from glory to glory, even as by the Spirit of the Lord" (2 Corinthians 3:18, literal translation). The pure in heart have nothing to hide, nothing to defend, nothing to explain. Their faces are unveiled. They advance "from glory to glory" until that day when they see Christ and become eternally like Him.

When you start to see God, you also start to see what God sees. You begin to see yourself in the light of God's glory. Abraham stood and talked with the Lord and called himself "nothing but dust and ashes" (Genesis 18:27). Job saw God and said, "Therefore

I despise myself and repent in dust and ashes" (Job 42:6). Peter fell down at Jesus' feet and said, "Go away from me, Lord; for I am a sinful man!" (Luke 5:8). Paul saw himself as "less than the least of all God's people" (Ephesians 3:8) and the "worst" of sinners (1 Timothy 1:15). The vision of God humbles a person. "So I was left alone, gazing at this great vision," wrote Daniel (10:8). "I had no strength left, my face turned deathly pale and I was helpless." Spiritual sight leads to spiritual insight. Isaiah saw the Lord and cried, "Woe to me! I am ruined" (Isaiah 6:5).

You not only see yourself in a new light, but you also see others in a new light. When the scribes and Pharisees looked at the publicans and sinners, they saw them as rebels, but Jesus saw them as lost coins, lost sheep, and lost children. The Pharisees saw God as a judge to condemn these rebels, but Jesus saw God as a seeking shepherd and a waiting father. The Pharisees saw Jesus as a glutton and a drunk, the friend of publicans and sinners. Jesus saw Himself as a physician who had come to heal the brokenhearted. It is impossible to divorce our vision of God and our insight into ourselves and others. If we would know each other, we must first know God.

The eyes see what the heart loves. If the heart loves God and is single in this devotion, then the eyes will see God whether others see Him or not. Nothing robs the heart of spiritual vision like sin. Saul's repeated disobedience blinded him to God, circumstances, Samuel, and David. Saul treated his enemies like friends and his friends like enemies. No wonder Paul prayed that the "eyes" of our understanding might be enlightened (Ephesians 1:18). Literally, it is "the eyes for your heart." Physically, our eyes tend to deteriorate, but spiritually our eyes ought to become keener and the vision brighter. If the light enters the body through the eyes and the "windows of the heart" become soiled, then the light grows dimmer and dimmer. Then we have to pray, with David, "Wash me" (Psalm 51:7).

The most important part of your life is the part only God sees. He knows whether your heart is pure. He wants your heart to be pure, for only then can you see God, and, in seeing God, receive all that He has and enjoy all that He is.

Blessed are the peacemakers,
for they will be called sons of God.
(MATTHEW 5:9)

The fruit of righteousness will be peace; the effect of
righteousness will be quietness and confidence forever.
(ISAIAH 32:17)

But the wisdom that comes from heaven is first of all pure;
then peace-loving, considerate, submissive, full of mercy
and good fruit, impartial and sincere.
(JAMES 3:17)

How good and pleasant it is when brothers
live together in unity!
(PSALM 133:1)

Let the peace of Christ rule in your hearts.
(COLOSSIANS 3:15)

But the fruit of the Spirit is love, joy, peace.
(GALATIANS 5:22)

9

THE PEACEMAKERS

The Bible is a book about peace. There are nearly four hundred references to peace in its pages, either personal peace with God or peace among people on an individual or a national level. The Bible opens and closes with peace, and the reason that there is a war in between is because of the opposition of Satan and the disobedience of people. God is not at war with the world, but the world is at war with God.

We must bear in mind that peace in the Bible is much more than the absence of war. There is no strife in a cemetery, but one would hardly use a cemetery as an example of peace. In the Bible, peace is a positive force; it signifies the presence of all that is good and wonderful. When two Jews meet or part from each other, they say, "Shalom! Peace!" but they mean much more than, "May you have no battles!" The word *shalom* contains in it a desire for all of the goodness that God can give, a total well-being for mind and heart and body. Peace is a creative force, and a peacemaker is a person who releases this creative force to change the world.

If you and I are to be peacemakers in a world filled with strife, then we must understand four basic truths about peace.

THE ORIGIN OF PEACE

The first truth is this: The source of peace is God. Six times in the New Testament He is called the God of peace. He is the God of peace as far as His person is concerned; there are no conflicts in the nature of God. You and I have battles within because we have a higher and a lower nature, but that is not so with God. His person is at perfect peace; His attributes harmoniously dwell and work together. God is at perfect peace with Himself, and that is why He is called the God of peace. One of the great Old Testament names for God is "Jehovah-shalom"—"the Lord Is Peace" (Judges 6:24).

Not only is He the God of peace as far as His person and His nature are concerned, but He is the God of peace as far as His will is concerned. "For I know the thoughts that I think toward you, says the Lord, thoughts of peace and not of evil, to give you a future and a hope" (Jeremiah 29:11 NKJV). God thinks about us; that in itself is a miracle. And the thoughts—the plans—that He thinks are for our peace, to accomplish a perfect purpose for our lives. The enemy would have us believe that God never thinks about us or that His thoughts are dangerous and painful. But such is not the case. God does think about us, and His thoughts point to peace.

He is the God of peace in the outworking of His will. Critics tell us that the Old Testament is certainly not a revelation of God, because its pages are filled with war and judgment. But if you read the Old Testament carefully, you discover that God's working is first peace, then war. The account of human history begins with peace, and it was only when humans sinned and joined with the enemy that God went to war. But even in His declaration of war there is the message of peace, the promise of the coming Redeemer (Genesis 3:15). The law of war that God gave to Israel in Deuteronomy 20 makes clear that Israel was to declare peace before it declared war. If the city refused to accept terms of peace, then Israel had to fight.

Our Lord Jesus Christ, the Prince of Peace, followed this same principle. At His birth, the angel announced, "on earth peace, to men" (Luke 2:14). There could have been peace on earth, had men received Him, but they said, "We don't want this man to be our king" (Luke 19:14).

How did Jesus respond to humanity's rejection of peace? "Do you think I came to bring peace on earth? No, I tell you, but division" (Luke 12:51). On that day when He rode into Jerusalem ("city of peace") and fulfilled the Old Testament prophecy, the city still would not receive Him. That was why He wept over the city, saying, "If you, even you, had only known on this day what would bring you peace—but now it is hidden from your eyes" (Luke 19:42). There was certainly no peace on earth.

Was there peace any place? Yes! The whole multitude of disciples rejoiced and praised God, saying, "Blessed is the king who comes in the name of the Lord! Peace in heaven and glory in the highest!" (Luke 19:38). Peace in heaven! There is no peace on earth, but there is peace in heaven, and that peace can be experienced on earth in the hearts of those who will yield to Christ.

Jesus Christ is God's peacemaker. "For he himself is our peace," wrote Paul in Ephesians 2:14, referring to Christ's work of uniting believing Jews and Gentiles into one body, the church. He made peace by His sacrificial death on the cross, and He preaches through His Spirit in the world today (Ephesians 2:15). As He faced the tortures of Calvary, Jesus was able to say to His disciples, "Peace I leave with you; my peace I give you" (John 14:27). "I have told you these things, so that in me you may have peace" (John 16:33).

Our God is the God of peace, and our Savior is the Prince of Peace. The Holy Spirit is the Spirit of peace, for it is He who applies and supplies the peace of God in our lives. "But the fruit of the Spirit is love, joy, peace" (Galatians 5:22). The source of peace is God; there is no other source. If you and I are going to be peacemakers, we must know God and draw upon His supply of peace.

THE OPPOSITION TO PEACE

The enemy of peace is sin. This is the second truth that believers must lay hold of if they are going to be peacemakers; otherwise, they will misunderstand what happens when people reject their peace. Jesus Christ is the Prince of Peace, yet three times in John's gospel we are told that there was division because of Him (7:43; 9:16; 10:19). "He stirs up the people" was one of the accusations at His trial (Luke 23:5). The apostle Paul was God's ambassador of peace, yet men said of him, "We have found this man to be a troublemaker" (Acts 24:5). Isaiah 32:17 promises, "The fruit of righteousness will be peace," but it seems that those who "hunger and thirst after righteousness" sometimes are the cause of war. "In fact, everyone who wants to live a godly life in Christ Jesus will be persecuted" (2 Timothy 3:12).

According to James 4:1–4, there are three wars going on in our world today.

What causes fights and quarrels among you? Don't they come from your desires that battle within you? You want something but don't get it. You kill and covet, but you cannot have what you want. You quarrel and fight. You do not have, because you do not ask God. When you ask, you do not receive, because you ask with wrong motives, that you may spend what you get on your pleasures. You adulterous people, don't you know that friendship with the world is hatred toward God? Anyone who chooses to be a friend of the world becomes an enemy of God.

People are at war with each other because they are at war with themselves ("your desires that battle within you"); they are not at war with themselves because they are at war with God. God has His enemies: the world (v. 4), the flesh (v. 1), and the devil (v. 7); whoever sides with these enemies declares war on God. Whenever you declare war on God, you become a troublemaker, not a peacemaker.

This helps to explain why so much trouble results when a Christian gets out of the will of God. Abraham tried to escape the famine in Canaan by going to Egypt, and there he created so many problems that the ruler had to ask him to leave (Genesis 12). Lot fell in love with Sodom, and the result was a conflict between Abraham and him (Genesis 13). David committed adultery with Bathsheba and brought tragic discipline down upon both his family and the nation. Jonah disobeyed God and created a storm that almost wrecked the ship and sent an unsaved, pagan crew out into a lost eternity. A believer living in sin is a great troublemaker, because sin is the enemy of peace.

At the same time, a believer living a godly life can be a cause of trouble. Why? Because a peacemaker reveals the war that is going on in the lives of unsaved people. Stephen's calmness as he faced his accusers only incited their hatred all the more. "I am a man of peace; but when I speak, they are for war" (Psalm 120:7). It has often been said that wherever Paul went, the result was either a revival or a riot, and sometimes it was both. "These men who have caused trouble all over the world have now come here"(Acts 17:6).

As long as people's hearts are sinful, there is going to be war in the world. The only solution is righteousness.

This explains why "Blessed are the pure in heart" precedes "Blessed are the peacemakers." Only the pure in heart can be peacemakers. "The work of righteousness will be peace; and the effect of righteousness, quietness and assurance forever" (Isaiah 32:17 NKJV). "But the wisdom that comes from heaven is first of all pure; then peace-loving . . . Peacemakers who sow in peace raise a harvest of righteousness" (James 3:17a–18). If I am at war with God because there is sin in my life, then I cannot be a peacemaker. It was Abraham who made peace, not Lot. Lot was a friend of the world and therefore the enemy of God, whereas Abraham was a friend of God and therefore the enemy of the world. Abraham sowed peace, and his descendants have been a channel of peace in the world. Lot sowed sin, and his descendants (the Ammonites and the Moabites, Genesis 19:36–38) were the enemies of Israel throughout history.

God's throne is a righteous throne, and His scepter is a scepter of righteousness. If we are going to reign in life, then we must deal with sin in our lives. Grace reigns "through righteousness" (Romans 5:21). Jesus Christ is "King of Righteousness" (Melchizedek) and "King of Peace" (Salem). In Him, "righteousness and peace kiss each other" (Psalm 85:10). David was a man after God's own heart and sought, in spite of his failures, to have a righteous reign in obedience to God. Saul's throne was a throne of deceit and disobedience. Saul's own son Jonathan admitted, "My father has made trouble for the country" (1 Samuel 14:29). Even after Saul's death, "there was a long war between the house of Saul and the house of David" (2 Samuel 3:1 KJV) until all the tribes of Israel crowned David their rightful king. These things are an allegory.

Until we crown Jesus Christ king in our lives and the Spirit puts sin to death, we can never be peacemakers.

THE OUTFLOW OF PEACE

The source of peace is God, and the enemy of peace is sin. The third truth is the minister of peace is the Christian. The angels can come and announce, "Peace on earth!" but they can never minister as peacemakers simply because they have never personally experienced the peace of God. We have experienced it, and therefore we can share it. "At one time we too were foolish, disobedient, deceived and enslaved by all kinds of passions and pleasures. We lived in malice and envy, being hated and hating one another" (Titus 3:3). But we came to the cross where Jesus Christ made peace, and there we found forgiveness for our sins. "Therefore, since we have been justified through faith, we have peace with God through our Lord Jesus Christ" (Romans 5:1). The war is now over, and because we are no longer at war with God, we are no longer at war with ourselves. "And the peace of God, which transcends all understanding" (Philippians 4:7) moves into our hearts and minds, and we are at peace with ourselves. Having received peace with God and having experienced the peace of God, we are now ready to be peacemakers. We are reigning in life because the peace of God is ruling in our hearts (Colossians 3:15).

We begin this ministry of peace by making peace with our brothers and sisters, and this starts with controlling anger (Matthew 5:21–26). Hatred in the heart is the equivalent of murder, and it begins with anger. More important than bringing a gift to the altar is getting right with my brother or sister so I can bring my gift with a heart that is right with God. Worship and warfare cannot exist at the same altar. "Settle matters quickly with your adversary" (Matthew 5:25) does not suggest cowardice or compromise. Rather, it suggests that we start with the positive before we deal with the negative; it means finding where I agree with my adversary before I discuss our areas of disagreement. When there is war in my heart, I should always look for points of agreement.

In the early years of my ministry, whenever others approached me with criticism, I usually lit into them and tried to change their mind. Then I learned to agree with my critics quickly, to find someplace where we could stand together and then from that place move into a constructive discussion of the problem. The words "Yes, I agree with you" have a way of disarming people and softening the blow. If you are out to win an argument, you will never agree with your adversary, but if you are out to win a brother, you will begin by declaring peace and not war.

Our Lord amplifies this matter in Matthew 18:15–17, where He instructs us to visit the estranged person privately and seek to win him or her back. If this fails, then take one or two others with you, and if that fails, it is necessary to take it to the church. The lesson is obvious: The longer a person delays in dealing with sin, the larger the influence of that sin grows. First, the sin involves only two people; then four are involved; and then the whole assembly of believers. "An offended brother is more unyielding than a fortified city" (Proverbs 18:19). But Proverbs 16:32 tells us, "Better a patient man than a warrior, a man who controls his temper than one who takes a city." If I am reigning in life through Christ and if I have His peace within, then I can storm the city and win the battle in love.

As peacemakers, we are also to seek to bring peace to our enemies. The instructions in Matthew 5:38–48 are both demanding and disturbing. Certainly the Lord was not giving a set of rules to follow on every occasion; otherwise, He was contradicting other admonitions in Scripture. It seems that He was describing an attitude of heart that is willing to suffer pain and loss if it will lead to the winning of an enemy. At least this is the interpretation Paul gave to the passage: "Do not take revenge, my friends, but leave room for God's wrath, for it is written: 'It is mine to avenge; I will repay,' says the Lord. On the contrary: 'If your enemy is hungry, feed him; if he is thirsty, give him something to drink. In doing this, you will heap burning coals on his head.' Do not be overcome by evil, but overcome evil with good" (Romans 12:19–21). Whatever rules my life, I will try to use to rule the lives of others, and whatever I use to control others will ultimately control me. To be sure, I may not be able to win every brother or convert every enemy. "If it is possible, as far as it depends on you, live at peace with everyone" (Romans 12:18). Sometimes it is not possible. But we must not give up too soon.

As peacemakers, we must never compromise just to bring about peace. "Peace at any price" is never right in the life of the believer. Peace at the expense of honesty and humility will only lead to more war. The quieting of the surface when the depths are still stormy is no lasting solution to the problem. "They dress the wound of my people as though it were not serious. 'Peace, peace,' they say, when there is no peace" (Jeremiah 6:14). The false prophets in Ezekiel's day whitewashed the tottering walls and pretended that the situation was in safe hands. "Because they lead my people astray, saying, 'Peace,' when there is no peace, and because, when a flimsy wall is built, they cover it with whitewash" (Ezekiel 13:10). A false peace is more dangerous than an open war because the problems have only been covered over. It is honesty, not hypocrisy, which makes for peace. "But the wisdom that comes from heaven is first of all pure; then peace-loving" (James 3:17).

Calvary is the greatest example of making peace. On the cross, God openly admitted the fact of sin. The horror of sin was not glossed over when Jesus died for the sins of the world. Instead of hiding sin, the Lord openly exposed it. But then He suffered for our sin. And because of His sacrifice, we are forgiven and we can be forgiving. We need never fear to deal with sin because it has already been dealt with at Calvary. The cross was His throne, and Jesus reigned as king when He made peace by the blood of His cross. His scepter had been a reed, and His crown was made of thorns, but He reigned just the same. As believers we, too, reign in life whenever we honestly and humbly deal with sin as we seek to win our fellow believer or our enemy.

There is a price to pay. Is it worth it?

THE OUTCOME OF PEACE

Yes, it is worth it, for the blessing of peace is godliness: "They will be called sons of God." The Father is the great peacemaker, and when you and I become peacemakers, we become like our Father. Beginning with the fifth Beatitude, the blessings bestowed are nothing less than attributes of God: mercy, purity in heart, peace. Children are like their parents, and as peacemakers, we become more like the Father in heaven.

This fact is certainly illustrated in the lives of Saul and David. As time passed, Saul became more and more of a troublemaker, and David did all he could to bring about peace. On two occasions David could have killed Saul, but David knew that this was not the way to deal with an enemy. In fact, when David cut off a part of Saul's robe, his heart "smote him" (1 Samuel 24:5 KJV), so sensitive was he to God's will. When one of David's men urged him to kill Saul, David replied, "As surely as the Lord lives," he said, "the Lord himself will strike him; either his time will come and he will die, or he will go into battle and perish" (1 Samuel 26:10). David knew that vengeance belongs to God. Because the peace of God controlled David's heart, the power of God controlled David's hand, and he did not use either the sword or the spear to destroy his enemy.

If any man was transformed from a troublemaker into a peacemaker, it was Saul of Tarsus. The very air that he breathed was "murderous threats" (Acts 9:1). He knew the law, but the law could neither change nor control him. When he saw Stephen die with glory on his face and a prayer of forgiveness on his lips, Saul never forgot it. Years later, he told that hushed Jewish crowd in the temple, "And when the blood of your martyr Stephen was shed, I stood there giving my approval and guarding the clothes of those who were killing him" (Acts 22:20). Saul of Tarsus the slave beheld Stephen the king, reigning in life and reigning in death. (The name *Stephen* means "crown.")

But unlike his namesake, Saul of Tarsus admitted his need and one day fell to his face and yielded to Jesus Christ. Here are two Sauls from Benjamin, both of whom fell, yet King Saul's fall meant defeat and death, and for Saul of Tarsus it meant victory and life. In the years that followed his conversion, Saul, "who is Paul," became a minister of reconciliation and an ambassador of peace, and eventually he paid for his ministry with his life. But it was worth it all, because Paul came to know Christ and become more like Him, even though he saw himself as "less than the least of all God's people" (Ephesians 3:8) and the "worst" of sinners (1 Timothy 1:15).

Hatred can never be conquered with hatred. Only love can conquer hatred. And when love declares war on hatred, the battle is always a difficult one. Love is like the light and reveals the darkness in hearts. Love challenges the enemy to be a better person, and this love often makes the conflict worse, because no person wants to admit that he or she is less than the enemy. The quiet calmness and pitying love of our Lord when they arrested and tried Him must have infuriated His enemies. The contrast between their brittle religious piety and His living, loving righteousness was too much for them, so they had to destroy Him. But a peacemaker cannot really be destroyed because the source of peace is God, and God is eternal. Jesus Christ arose from the dead, and today He shares His peace with all who will "kiss the Son" (Psalm 2:12) and trust in Him.

David and Solomon illustrate two aspects of this matter of peace. David was a man of war, because peace is not purchased cheaply. Solomon was a man of peace, and under his reign Israel reached its greatest heights of glory and prosperity. But Solomon built upon the victories his father had won. Jesus Christ is the Prince of Peace, but He had to fight that awesome battle against sin by dying on the cross. "And through him to reconcile to himself all things, whether things on earth or things in heaven, by making peace through his blood, shed on the cross" (Colossians 1:20). Solomon built the temple because David won the battles, and in each we see the peace work of our Lord Jesus Christ.

As you and I seek to be peacemakers, people will treat us as they did Jesus. They will misunderstand us and not honestly seek for the truth. They will criticize us and accuse us. Eventually they will condemn us and crucify us. Hatred blinds, whereas love sharpens vision. Hatred looks for a victim, whereas love seeks a victory. The person of war throws stones, and the peacemaker builds a bridge out of those stones. The person of war comes with a sword, and the peacemaker disarms him or her with love and beats that sword into a plowshare. The person of war throws a spear, and the peacemaker beats it into a pruning hook. Peacemakers do not avoid the battle; instead, they transform the battle into a ministry of reconciliation. How do they do this? Certainly not in their own strength! "God has poured out his love into our hearts by the Holy Spirit, whom he has given us" (Romans 5:5). "But the fruit of the Spirit is . . . peace" (Galatians 5:22).

*Blessed are those who are persecuted because of righteous-
ness, for theirs is the kingdom of heaven. Blessed are you
when people insult you, persecute you and falsely say all
kinds of evil against you because of me. Rejoice and be glad,
because great is your reward in heaven, for in the same way
they persecuted the prophets who were before you.*
(MATTHEW 5:10–12)

*Woe to you when all men speak well of you, for that
is how their fathers treated the false prophets.*
(LUKE 6:26)

*Dear friends, do not be surprised at the painful trial you are
suffering, as though something strange were happening to you.
But rejoice that you participate in the sufferings of Christ,
so that you may be overjoyed when his glory is revealed.*
(1 PETER 4:12–13)

*The apostles left the Sanhedrin, rejoicing because they had
been counted worthy of suffering disgrace for the Name.*
(ACTS 5:41)

If you falter in times of trouble, how small is your strength!
(PROVERBS 24:10)

10

THE PERSECUTED

There is a brand of Christianity today that seems unlike the kind that Jesus spoke about in the Gospels and that Paul spoke about in the epistles. It is an easygoing, popular kind of religion that is acceptable to the world because it involves no conviction and no cross, or at least no cross as Jesus spoke of it. When He told the crowds that they had to take up a cross in order to be His disciples, the crowds left Him and eventually killed Him. Humankind has no problem accepting and following a religious leader who permits them to stay in their sins, but they will crucify the man who dares to point them to a narrow gate that leads to a narrow way. Even Peter was amazed that following Jesus involved a cross. "Never, Lord!" he said. "This shall never happen to you!" (Matthew 16:22).

I met a Christian friend one day whom I had not seen in several years, and he was telling me his experiences as a Christian. "By the way," he remarked, "the last time I heard you preach, you talked about Christians being persecuted. I'll have to confess to you that I don't agree with you. I have never been persecuted for being a Christian, and I don't believe it's a necessary part of the Christian life."

We had to part company just then, but had we remained together I would have pointed out to him that the righteous have always suffered for their faith in one way or another. It began with

Abel's being killed by Cain—and Cain was a religious man, by the way. Moses chose "to be mistreated along with the people of God " (Hebrews 11:25) rather than to compromise in Egypt. Jesus Himself told us that the prophets were persecuted. The book of Acts and all of church history since then verify our Lord's prediction. "In fact, everyone who wants to live a godly life in Christ Jesus will be persecuted" (2 Timothy 3:12).

REASONS FOR PERSECUTION

The reasons for persecution are not difficult to understand. Jesus names two: We are persecuted "because of righteousness" and for His name's sake. We must be careful to distinguish between persecution and punishment. Good people punish us for doing evil, and bad people persecute us for doing good. Peter knew the difference: "If you are insulted because of the name of Christ, you are blessed . . . If you suffer, it should not be as a murderer or thief or any other kind of criminal, or even as a meddler. However, if you suffer as a Christian, do not be ashamed, but praise God that you bear that name" (1 Peter 4:14–16).

Sad to say, some believers do not know the difference between being offensive and "the offense of the cross" (Galatians 5:11) or between being witnesses and being prosecuting attorneys. Jesus used the world *falsely*, and it is an important word. If I get into trouble because I talk too much or because I meddle or because I try to force my faith on other people, that is not persecution. If I am promoting my own cause and people reject me, that is not persecution. If I am arrogant and abusive in my attempt to witness for Christ and people want nothing to do with me, that is not persecution. But if I seek to do His will and honor His name and as a result I suffer, then that is persecution.

Some believers have an ego problem and want to be noticed and praised, so they deliberately get themselves into trouble in order to claim that they have been persecuted for the Lord. Christians who are devotedly carrying their crosses never have to manufacture persecution. If we live the way Jesus lived, then the world will treat us the way it treated Him, and we will share in "the fellowship of his sufferings" (Philippians 3:10).

True persecution comes "because of righteousness." It is the result of the believer's daring to live the Beatitudes. The world's philosophy is exactly opposite of that which Jesus expresses in the Beatitudes, and these opposite viewpoints lead to opposing ways of life. The narrow road that we walk is not parallel to the broad road; it runs right down the middle. We are walking in one direction and the world is walking in the other, and it is impossible not to collide. Jesus tells us to be "poor in spirit," but the world tells us to build up our egos and be important. Humility is not a virtue that is admired in today's society. In fact, unbelievers look upon humility as a form of weakness. George Bernard Shaw stated their position perfectly when he said, "Leave it to the coward to make a religion of his cowardice by preaching humility."

Neither is the world interested in mourning over sin. Unbelievers will quickly regret the uncomfortable effects of sin, but even that passes away. Meekness they consider weakness because, after all, it is the aggressive person who gets ahead in this world. "Winner take all, and the devil take the hindmost!" The world has no appetite for righteousness. Its motto is "Eat, drink, and be merry, for tomorrow we die!" Mercy—purity of heart—and peacemaking are concepts that are rarely, if ever, found in the mind of the unbeliever. To show mercy when your enemy is under your sword's point is to lose the victory. Such is "the counsel of the wicked" (Psalm 1:1).

The root meaning of the word *righteousness* is "to divide, to be different." "If you belonged to the world, it would love you as its own. As it is, you do not belong to the world, but I have chosen you out of the world. That is why the world hates you" (John 15:19). The holy Son of God was a cause of division when He was in the world, and those who seek to live like Him will produce the same results. "If they persecuted me," said Jesus, "they will persecute you also" (John 15:20b). Jesus was different, and a world that thrives on conformity cannot tolerate differences. We are children of light, and they are children of darkness. We are alive in the Spirit, and they are dead in sins. We live by faith, and they live by sight. We understand them, but they do not understand us.

We are persecuted because of righteousness and "because of my name, for they do not know the One who sent me" (John 15:21). The Lord came to earth to reveal God's name to us (John 17:6). Because the world doesn't know God, it doesn't know His Son, Jesus Christ; ignorance breeds suspicion, and suspicion breeds fear. People tend to attack whatever they fear. That explains why sinful men killed God's Son and now try to kill those who have trusted Him. "For it has been granted to you on behalf of Christ not only to believe on him, but also to suffer for him"(Philippians 1:29). In this day of tolerance, let a person announce that he or she is a homosexual or an abortion rights supporter, and few people, if anybody, will get upset. But let a person announce that he or she is a Christian, let the name of Christ come into the conversation, and war is declared.

Persecution is a normal part of dedicated Christian living. It is not the thermostat of the Christian life. Our love for Christ is that. But it is the thermometer; it helps us measure how much we are like the Savior.

RESPONSES TO PERSECUTION

As believers, we must respond to persecution and not react. We need to be prepared with the right attitude of mind. "Therefore, since Christ suffered in his body, arm yourselves also with the same attitude, because he who has suffered in his body is done with sin" (1 Peter 4:1). A proper attitude of mind is a weapon in the battle against Satan. We do not react, then resent, and then retaliate. That is the way the world acts when difficulties come. No, believers respond in a positive way, not because they seek persecution but because they expect it and are not surprised when it comes. Jesus tells us that there are three proper responses: We reign (Matthew 5:10); we rejoice (Matthew 5:12); and we release love (Matthew 5:43–48).

"For theirs is the kingdom of heaven" simply means that believers reign in life in the midst of persecution. They act like kings, not slaves. The more King Saul persecuted David, the more David reigned in life through faith in God. David knew that he was the rightful king, for God had anointed David and promised him the throne. So he acted like a king. When he could have killed Saul, David exercised self-control and let him go free. When David could have slain Shimei for his stones and slanders, David ignored the man and left the matter with God. When you know you are a king, it is beneath your dignity to retaliate because that only makes you like other people.

On March 11, 1830, a British girl was doing her lessons with her tutor, and the lesson that day had to do with the royal family. As she studied the genealogical chart in the book, she became aware of the astounding fact that she was next in line for the throne. At first she wept, and then she looked at her tutor and said, "I will be good!" The fact that little Victoria would one day be queen motivated her to live on a higher level, and the fact that you and I are already kings should motivate us not to retaliate.

After all, there are only three levels on which we can live: the demonic, the human, and the divine. Satan returns evil for good; people return good for good and evil for evil; but God returns good for evil. "He causes his sun to rise on the evil and the good, and sends rain on the righteous and the unrighteous" (Matthew 5:45). People with low self-esteem quickly react and retaliate because they must defend themselves. But believers who know they are kings are so filled with God's riches that it is beneath their dignity to retaliate. Jesus could have summoned legions of angels, yet He willingly let sinful men slap Him in the face, spit upon Him, pluck out His beard, mock Him, and then crucify Him.

Our first response is to reign, and our second is to rejoice: "Rejoice and be glad" (Matthew 5:12). Impossible? The disciples did it when they were persecuted: "The apostles left the Sanhedrin, rejoicing because they had been counted worthy of suffering disgrace for the Name" (Acts 5:41). Years later, Peter wrote: "If you are insulted because of the name of Christ, you are blessed" (1 Peter 4:14). How is it possible for suffering people to rejoice? To begin with, we realize that it is a privilege to be persecuted for Jesus' sake. The persecution is evidence that we are living like Him and glorifying Him, and that ought to make any Christian rejoice. "The fellowship of his sufferings" (Philippians 3:10) is the closest fellowship possible; when we are in the furnace, the Son of God is there with us.

But something else makes us rejoice: We have new opportunities to witness for Christ. Our English word *martyr* is a transliteration of the Greek word that means "witness." Stephen suffered persecution, even to death, and one result was the conversion of Saul of Tarsus. When the world sees a godly believer rejoice in persecution, it realizes that the Christian life is something more than a mere religion. The greatest opportunities we have for witnessing come when the stones are flying.

Persecution also gives us an opportunity to grow. When the world praises us, we are in spiritual danger, but when the world persecutes us, we can be sure we are living for Christ and becoming more like Him. The furnace of suffering purges out the dross of sin. "He who has suffered in his body is done with sin. As a result, he does not live the rest of his earthly life for evil human desires, but rather for the will of God" (1 Peter 4:1b–2). Persecution has a way of driving us to God; it helps us examine our priorities and strengthen our spiritual roots. Suffering by itself never makes a person grow, but suffering in the will of God and for the glory of God is a great stimulus to spiritual development. "Before I was afflicted I went astray, but now I obey your word . . . It was good for me to be afflicted so that I might learn your decrees" (Psalm 119:67, 71).

This spiritual joy, of course, is not something that we work up; it is the gift of the Holy Spirit: "For the Spirit of glory and of God rests on you" (1 Peter 4:14). This joy comes from trusting and loving Christ. "Though you have not seen him, you love him; and even though you do not see him now, you believe in him and are filled with an inexpressible and glorious joy" (1 Peter 1:8). Even our Lord Jesus endured the cross because of "the joy set before him" (Hebrews 12:2).

We respond to persecution by reigning, rejoicing, and releasing love. "But I tell you: Love your enemies and pray for those who persecute you" (Matthew 5:44). This is the consequence of reigning and rejoicing.

Christian love is not a shallow sentiment; it is a settled attitude of the mind and heart that leads to definite actions of the will. Christian love means that I treat you the way God treats me.

This is why Jesus adds to His command to love our enemies, "that you may be sons of your Father in heaven" (Matthew 5:45). God loved us when we were His enemies, and He sent His Son to die for us. We should treat our enemies the way God has treated us—we should be patient, forgiving, and willing to sacrifice for their good, even though they may not deserve it.

If we have sincere Christian love, it will reveal itself in our prayers and our actions. We will pray for our enemies that they might come to know the Lord—not so that *our* way will be easier but so that *their* way will be easier. We need the kind of love Jesus showed when He prayed, "Father, forgive them, for they do not know what they are doing" (Luke 23:34). We need the kind of love Stephen showed when he prayed, "Lord Jesus, receive my spirit . . . Lord, do not hold this sin against them" (Acts 7:59–60). We do not need to pray that fire from heaven will consume our enemies (Luke 9:54–56).

But it is not enough to live and pray; we must act. By doing something positive for our enemies, we release God's love to touch their lives. This is what Paul meant when he said that we "heap burning coals on his head" (Romans 12:17–21). Our motives may be questioned and our ministries rejected, but for Jesus' sake we must do good to our enemies if ever they are going to experience the grace of God and become Christians. And even if they do not become Christians, we become better Christians for having done the will of God.

REWARDS OF PERSECUTION

There are definite rewards for the believer who suffers persecution in the will of God. Some people may believe that rewards are a poor motive for obedience, but Jesus did not think so. To be sure, character is reward enough, but in His grace, Jesus was willing to add something extra. And, after all, whatever rewards we receive only bring greater glory to Him, both here and hereafter.

There is a present reward stated: "For theirs is the kingdom of heaven" (Matthew 5:10). He was not talking about entering the kingdom, because that is covered in the first Beatitude. He was talking about enjoying the kingdom. When you are able to exercise self-control in the midst of persecution and pray for your persecutors and do good to them, then you have entered into the secrets of the throne and the riches of His glory. No matter how little we may have of material things, we enjoy God's spiritual riches as we reign in life through Jesus Christ. To be sure, there is a future reward, and the Lord names it, but right here and now we live like kings.

Another reward is our identification with Christ and the prophets: "For in the same way they persecuted the prophets who were before you" (Matthew 5:12). What a holy band of saints to belong to! Here were believers "of whom the world was not worthy" (Hebrews 11:38 KJV), and we are privileged to fellowship with them. A person's company is a great revealer of his or her character. "On their release, Peter and John went back to their own people" (Acts 4:23). While He was ministering on earth, Jesus was identified with the suffering prophets of old. "Some say John the Baptist; others say Elijah; and still others, Jeremiah or one of the prophets" (Matthew 16:14). All three of the men named were persecuted because of their faith and their faithfulness.

Today we can enter into the riches of the kingdom and the fellowship of the martyrs, but there is also a future reward: "Great is your reward in heaven" (Matthew 5:12). Never minimize the present power of a future reward. Moses turned his back on Egypt and suffered for it because "he was looking ahead to his reward" (Hebrews 11:26). Abraham walked by faith as he looked for that city God had promised him. Jesus encourages us today by promising us heavenly rewards tomorrow, and there is nothing wrong with this encouragement. "If we suffer, we shall also reign with him" (2 Timothy 2:12 KJV). One of the repeated themes of 1 Peter is suffering and glory; Peter wrote to encourage Christians going through fiery trials. It is easy for comfortable saints to despise promised rewards, but let them go into the fires and they might change their minds.

This is the last of the Beatitudes, the climax of them all. It is difficult to believe that people would persecute those who are humble and meek, who are seeking after righteousness, who are merciful and trying to make peace. But they do. The dedication of the saints only magnifies the depravity of the sinners.

The world welcomes a compromising Christian, but it hates the Christian who does the will of God. In some respects, this final Beatitude is the measure of the others. As we are growing in Christian character, we will experience more conflict. It is impossible to have one without the other.

We are never really finished with the Beatitudes because there are always new discoveries of our own hearts and of God's grace. We grow in grace as we grow in knowledge—knowledge of Christ and knowledge of ourselves. We reign in life, but there is always new territory to conquer and control. We enjoy the kingdom that we might enlarge the kingdom. Jesus dealt with this theme in His statement about salt and light.

You are the salt of the earth. But if the salt loses its saltiness, how can it be made salty again? It is no longer good for anything, except to be thrown out and trampled by men. You are the light of the world. A city on a hill cannot be hidden. Neither do people light a lamp and put it under a bowl. Instead they put it on its stand, and it gives light to everyone in the house. In the same way, let your light shine before men, that they may see your good deeds and praise your Father in heaven.
(MATTHEW 5:13–16)

11

THE SALT AND THE LIGHT

Salt and light are commodities that we take for granted, but in the ancient world they were greatly valued. Roman soldiers were given their salt rations and would revolt if those rations were changed. Our English word *salary* literally means "salt money." The next time you say, "That man is not worth his salt," you are reminding yourself of the value that people put on salt back in those days.

We flick a switch and have as much light as we need, but the Jews that Jesus ministered to had to carry little clay dishes with oil and wicks if they wanted light. When one of our cities experiences a power failure, we wake up to the fact that light is important, but usually we take it for granted.

Jesus used salt and light as pictures of the Christian. No doubt He was describing the disciples particularly, since He changed from using the third person in the Beatitudes to the second person in these verses. But to apply these truths only to the disciples would rob us of the blessing and rob the world of the ministry that every believer can perform. In the Beatitudes, our Lord was describing Christian character; now in these two illustrations He showed what this character means in everyday life. By using the images of salt and light, He gave us some valuable insights into what it means to be a Christian today.

THE WONDER OF SALVATION

He first gave us an insight into our own salvation. When we trusted Christ, a miracle took place. We became "[participants] in the divine nature" (2 Peter 1:4), so that a new ingredient was added to our lives. Clay became salt, and darkness became light: "For you were once darkness, but now you are light in the Lord" (Ephesians 5:8).

Christians are different from unbelievers because they possess the nature of God, having been born into His family. "God is light" (1 John 1:5), and we are the children of light. Throughout the ancient world, salt was a symbol of purity and faithfulness, and Jesus Christ dared to apply this symbol to those who trust Him. It must have shocked both the disciples and the crowd when Jesus gave them those titles. They could understand a king or a great prophet being called "the salt of the earth" and "the light of the world," but certainly not a group of ordinary laypeople. Still, it is true: Because of the miracle of God's grace, the Christian is salt and light. A new ingredient has been added, and an old ingredient has been taken away. Sin has been forgiven, the new nature has been implanted, and the Christian stands before the world as God's salt and light.

That means both privilege and responsibility. Along with the dignity of our calling is the duty of our calling. Jesus does not tell us that we should be salt and light; He tells us that we *are* salt and light. We cannot change what we are, but we can waste what we are—the salt can lose its saltiness, and the light can be put under a bowl. That does not deny the miracle that changed us; it only defeats the ministry that challenges us. It would do us good to reflect from time to time on the miracle of our salvation—that clay should become salt and darkness should become light. Taking for granted this miracle of God's grace is certain to lead to spiritual decay. The wonder and glory of it must never leave our hearts. Knowing that I am in Christ enables me, by faith, to do what Christ wants me to do.

The Sermon on the Mount is an impossible enigma to those who have never experienced this miracle. No matter how religious they may be or how sincere, if they have never been transformed by God's power, they can never live the transformed life described in this sermon. It requires a miracle.

THE PLIGHT OF THE WORLD

Those two images also give us insight into our world. If Christians are salt, then they are living in a *decaying* world, and if they are light, they are living in a *dark* world.

Jesus harbored no illusions about this world. To be sure, He saw His Father's creation and rejoiced in it—the lilies of the field, the sparrows, even the seeds in the sower's bag. Nowhere does the Bible condemn God's creation in spite of the fact that creation is groaning because of sin. The heavens still declare the glory of God, and the earth reveals His handiwork (Psalm 19:1). The world of creation is here for us to enjoy.

Neither did our Lord condemn the world of humanity. "For God so loved the world that he gave his one and only Son" (John 3:16). Sin has done terrible damage to the creature that God made in His image; but God still loves people and wants to save them. The world of creation and the world of humanity have both been ravaged by sin, but both can share in redemption. Humanity apart from Christ is lost, and Jesus came to save the lost.

It is the world that humanity has made that is decaying, that whole system that denies God and exalts itself. When Jesus said, "They are not of the world, even as I am not of it" (John 17:16), it was this system to which He was referring. We are in the world physically but not of the world spiritually. Like scuba divers in the ocean, believers are out of their element in this present world system because their citizenship is in heaven. The world is a vast graveyard spiritually, and Christians are the only people who are really alive. Jesus looked upon the world as a decaying corpse when He said, "Where there is a dead body, there the vultures will gather" (Luke 17:37). And Peter described this world system as "a dark place" (2 Peter 1:19). The word translated *dark* means "squalid" or "murky," which hardly pictures this world as a paradise.

Death, of course, causes decay. When a living creature dies, it can no longer support its cell structure, so the body begins to decompose. When God created the world and the first man and woman, everything pulsated with life. When sin invaded, death entered the scene, and with death came decay. From a physical point of view, decay became a blessing because it removes unwanted dead matter and turns it into useful soil, but from a spiritual point of view, decay is disaster. It is evidence of a spiritual death: Humanity is separated from God.

We see decay in every area of life. Centuries ago, the prophet Daniel saw the meaning of the image and revealed the fact that the political world would decay—from gold to silver, to brass, and then to iron and clay (Daniel 2). History started with clay, and it will end with clay. Certainly the religious world is decaying; humans have a "form of godliness," but there is no power (2 Timothy 3:5). "However, when the Son of Man comes, will he find faith on the earth?" (Luke 18:8). One does not have to take a survey to learn that moral standards have decayed. The "terrible times" that Paul warned about are certainly here (2 Timothy 3:1–5).

When things decay they fall apart, and we are seeing society fall apart around us. Marriages have a difficult time staying together, and families are scattered. Law and order are laughed at, and the basic institutions of society are threatened with extinction. On the outside some of the structures look sound, but inside they are rotting away, and it is only a matter of time before they fall. The corpse is rotting away, and the eagles are gathering together.

Not only is it a decaying world but also it is a dark world, in spite of the fact that we claim to be enlightened. There is a great deal of knowledge and little wisdom. Intellectual darkness pervades our public educational systems because God has been denied admittance. "For although they knew God, they neither glorified him as God nor gave thanks to him, but their thinking became futile and their foolish hearts were darkened" (Romans 1:21). History is not an account of evolution, with humanity climbing higher; it is a sad tale of devolution, with humanity turning its back on the heights and plunging to the depths. People are not looking for the light; they have rejected the light and are walking in the shadows into deeper and deeper darkness. Humanity's very light is darkness! "If then the light within you is darkness, how great is that darkness!" (Matthew 6:23).

Darkness and decay go together. Because there is political darkness, the governments of the world are decaying. Because there is religious darkness, the religions of the world are falling apart and desperately trying to save themselves by joining together. And because there is moral darkness, it is not safe to walk the streets even in the daytime. "See, darkness covers the earth and thick darkness is over the peoples" (Isaiah 60:2).

This darkness and decay help to explain why people are confused. Nothing looks right in the dark. You can see shapes but not sizes and appearances. Everything is distorted in the dark. Is it any wonder that values are twisted and distorted with the world so shrouded in darkness? Gold is more important than goodness, things are more important than people, and God is not important at all. No wonder people stumble and fall. No wonder people cannot tell their friends from their enemies. When Jesus Christ was on earth, the light was shining. "While I am in the world, I am the light of the world" (John 9:5). He warned them: "You are going to have the light just a little while longer. Walk while you have the light, before darkness overtakes you. The man who walks in the dark does not know where he is going" (John 12:35).

Is there any hope for a dark, decaying world?

THE CHALLENGE OF MINISTRY

The third insight that our Lord gave us is into our own position and ministry in this world. The world is decaying, but Christians are salt. The world is dark, but Christians are light.

Salt, of course, hinders corruption. The fact that the world is decaying should not encourage Christians to isolate and insulate themselves or to stand on the sidelines and wait for the great collapse. The contrast between Jonah and Jesus illustrates this point: Jonah sat outside the city and hoped that judgment would fall, whereas Jesus looked upon the city and wept over it because judgment was inevitable. Sometimes we Christians not only hate sin—we hate sinners! Abraham knew how corrupt Sodom was, yet he prayed that the city might be spared. Paul knew how blind Israel was, yet he was willing to be accursed that Israel might be saved. Joseph in Egypt and Daniel in Babylon both acted as divine salt in the midst of a corrupt society, and God used them. Their ministries did not prevent the ultimate collapse of the nations, but those men did stand for God and left the nations without excuse.

If the world is as corrupt as it is with Christians present in it, what will civilization be like when the Christians are gone? Little does the world system realize that it is the presence of God's people that prevents that final collapse and that ultimate judgment. Lot was anything but a dedicated believer, yet his presence in Sodom made it impossible for God to judge the city. His presence in Zoar spared the city; his absence from Sodom condemned the city. One day God will judge this present world system, but He must call His own out of it before that judgment can fall. Meanwhile, our responsibility is to exert all the power we can to prevent decay and to win people to Christ. That does not mean that we must live like the world in order to influence the world. Abraham, separated from Sodom, actually had more influence on the city than did Lot, who was living in Sodom. And he did the city more good! When the kings captured Lot and the rest of the citizens, it was Abraham who rescued them. By risking his life to save them, Abraham gave them more witness in one night than Lot had given them in years. And when Abraham refused to accept the offer of the king of Sodom, he witnessed to the whole city that his faith was in the true God. Lot, immersed in the activities of the sinful city, had no influence upon his own family, yet Abraham, the friend of God, exerted a powerful influence as he interceded for the lost.

Salt not only hinders corruption, but it also seasons whatever it touches. The world is a better place for the presence of Christians, whether the world admits it or not. If we were to take out of civilization the influence of Christian thought and Christian people, little would be left. This is not to say that only Christians have made lasting contributions to society, because many unbelievers have contributed much that is of value. But it is because of the fruits of the Christian message that humanity has the freedom and the dignity to pursue truth. Even modern science, which may scoff at the gospel, is a result of the gospel. When God gave man dominion, He gave His mandate to search and discover and invent.

The furniture of the house of civilization comes from many different hands, but God laid the foundation.

When salt touches an open wound, it stings. Christians are not honey to soothe a sinful world; they are salt to convict it. The presence of the Holy Spirit in the church, witnessing through the world, convicts the world "of guilt in regard to sin and righteousness and judgment" (John 16:8). That is one reason the world hates Christians. "If I had not come and spoken to them, they would not be guilty of sin. Now, however, they have no excuse for their sin" (John 15:22).

Salt makes people thirsty. If we are truly the salt of the earth, people will see in us what they are seeking for themselves and will want to take hold of it. Jesus attracted all kinds of needy people— and so should the dedicated Christian. The lost may not agree with our theology or even our way of life, but they will see in us qualities that they lack themselves and would like to possess. The Pharisees repelled the publicans and sinners, but Jesus attracted them. He made them thirsty for what He alone could give. The more we are like Him, the more sinners will be attracted by our life and witness as we are the salt of the earth.

But we are also the light of the world. Jesus defined this light as "good works." As salt, we must have the kind of character that penetrates and purifies, and as light, we must have the kind of conduct that points to God. We like to think of these good works as religious works, but Jesus did not define them that way. Good works are simply works motivated by love, energized by the Spirit, and done to the glory of God. "For it is God who works in you to will and to act according to his good purpose" (Philippians 2:13). Unsaved people certainly can perform good deeds, but these are not like the Spirit-directed good works that come from the lives of

God's people. Too often good deeds point to the doer, but the good works Jesus talked about point to God.

Once again, we must avoid extremes. There are those who believe they have not served God unless they have preached a sermon or given out a piece of Christian literature. There are others who reject that kind of service and think only of the "practical" things of life, such as healing the sick and feeding the hungry. Social action sometimes replaces evangelism. Actually, our good works glorify God only if they begin with God and are empowered by His Spirit. Jesus said of the Holy Spirit, "He will bring glory to me" (John 16:14). Whether we are giving a neighbor a ride to the store, helping a child with his or her lessons, or teaching a Sunday school class, if our works are motivated by love and empowered by the Spirit, they will point others to God. There are no such categories as religious works and secular works, for the Christian is to "do it all for the glory of God" (1 Corinthians 10:31). Missionary doctors heal the body that they might demonstrate God's love and eventually have the privilege of helping to heal the soul. Christian neighbors help those around them, not simply to win the right to be heard but because showing Christian love is in itself a ministry to the glory of God.

Salt and light balance each other. Salt is hidden; it works secretly and slowly. Light is seen; it works openly and quickly. The influence of Christian character is quiet and penetrating. The influence of Christian conduct is obvious and attracting. The two go together and reinforce each other. Conduct without character is hypocrisy; character without conduct is disobedience. A church officer once told me, "I don't go around the shop doing a lot of good works. I just let my light shine for the Lord." But the way to let your light shine is to do good works. And those good works must be backed up with true character, the kind that is described in the Beatitudes.

Both salt and light must make contact if they are to do any good. Salt in the container can never have any influence; neither can a light hidden under a bowl. Too many Christians have the idea that they are serving God by sitting in church when the greatest needs are outside the church building. We fellowship with God's people that we might receive the grace needed to serve Christ out in the world. Worship builds character, and character leads to conflict. Separation from sin does not mean isolation from sinners. The salt must make contact if it is to do any good, and the light must be seen. Why is it that so few believers dare to make this contact? The answer to that question leads us to the fourth insight that Jesus gave us.

THE DANGERS AHEAD

The Lord gave us insight into the dangers that are involved when you and I attempt to be salt and light in this world. There is, first of all, the danger that the salt might lose its saltiness and become good for nothing. Our modern salt doesn't lose its flavor because it is highly refined, but back in Jesus' day, salt did lose its flavor. William Thompson, in his classic work *The Land and the Book*, tells about a merchant who rented several houses in which he stored salt. The merchant, however, forgot to cover the dirt floors of the houses and simply unloaded the salt directly on the earth. When he returned many days later, he discovered that his salt had lost its flavor from being next to the ground. The entire supply was actually thrown into the street, where people walked on it.

Christians are not yet perfect; there is still that old nature within that can cause them to sin. The greatest problem we face in serving Christ is having contact with sinners without being contaminated by sin. Jesus Christ was the friend of publicans and sinners, yet He was "holy, blameless, pure, set apart from sinners, exalted above the heavens" (Hebrews 7:26). There was contact without contamination; there was true separation without insulation or isolation. Only the Spirit of God can keep us from losing our flavor as we seek to minister to the lost. Of course, this loss of flavor would be a gradual thing. First there is friendship with the world (James 4:4), and then we are spotted by the world (see James 1:27). This leads to a love for the world (1 John 2:15) and then conformity to the world (Romans 12:2). By then, the salt has lost its flavor and is good for nothing.

We must also beware of the light's being hidden. Only we can hide our lights. The religious leaders tried to hide the lights of the apostles, but the more the lights were threatened, the brighter they blazed. The history of the church is the story of the light shining in the darkness and the darkness trying to put it out (John 1:5). Our Lord was not talking about people losing their salvation, because such an experience is not possible. His subject was witnessing, glorifying God by the lives that we live. Unless the oil of the Holy Spirit feeds the wick of witness, the light will go out. "But you shall receive power, when the Holy Ghost is come upon you, and you shall be witnesses unto me" (Acts 1:8, literal translation).

It is worth noting that Jesus put the lamp on the lamp stand ("candlestick") where it could give light "to all the house." If our light is going to shine at all, it will shine first at home. The man out of whom Jesus cast the legion of demons wanted to go with the Lord and serve Him, but Jesus told him: "Go home to your family and tell them how much the Lord has done for you, and how he has had mercy on you" (Mark 5:19). We think that the greatest darkness is the farthest away, when it may be right at home. And the light that shines brightly at home will reach people away from home.

In these days of mass movements and great organizations, we tend to belittle the witness of one person. "What can a little salt do to influence a whole world?" we ask. "What good is a little candle when the world is so dark?" And yet the emphasis in the Bible is on the work and witness of *one person*. When human history was at its darkest after the flood, God called one man, Abraham, and this one man has blessed the whole world. When Israel was experiencing its darkest hour in Egypt, God called one man, Moses, and the result was freedom. God has always had His person waiting in the wings when it seemed impossible for the drama of history to finish on a note of victory.

God is still looking for people who will be salt and light. It is a difficult and dangerous ministry, but it is an essential one. Salt and light must give of themselves so that others might be helped, and what they do is usually taken for granted. But whether the salt and light are praised is really not important. The important thing is that people glorify God.

NOTE TO THE READER

The publisher invites you to share your response to the message of this book by writing Discovery House Publishers, Box 3566, Grand Rapids, MI 49501, USA. For information about other Discovery House books, music, or videos, contact us at the same address or call 1-800-653-8333. Find us on the Internet at http://www.dhp.org/ or send e-mail to books@dhp.org.